Information

Communication and Society

INFORMATION

Communication and Society

AJAY PRATAP SINGH
Head & Associate Professor
Department of library & information science
Banaras Hindu University
&
MAYANK YUVARAJ
Junior Research Fellow
Department of library & information science
Banaras Hindu University

Ess Ess Publications
New Delhi

***INFORMATION:* Communication and Society**

ISBN: 978-81-7000-693-0

First Published 2013

Published by:
Ess Ess Publications
4831/24, Ansari Road,
Darya Ganj,
New Delhi-110 002.
INDIA
Phones: 23260807, 41563444
Fax: 41563334
E-mail: info@essessreference.com
www.essessreference.com

Cover Design by *Patch Creative Unit*

Printed and bound in India at Salasar Imaging Systems.

"When the going gets tough the tough get going."

To the
Service and Commitment
of
Information Profession

Contents

Preface

The centrality of information profession lies in providing right information at right place at right time. The discipline of Information Science has matured over the past decade. The new focus of information professionals lies in serving people with appropriate content and contexts accessible via new Medias. The idea of providing readers with one book at one time is no longer feasible. While the core of the profession has remained the same the responsibilities and nature have changed. The centrality of information practises rests on principles and philosophies derived from scientific premises that lend the subject a scientific edge. There was a need to condense the concepts involving the dynamics of information and information phenomena to provide a comprehensive theoretical base which prompted to write this book.

WHO SHOULD READ THIS BOOK?

This book explains some of the nuts and bolts of the information science and the profession. On the front lines, the intended readers of this book are the Library & Information Science professionals seeking professional development and students at Graduate/ Post-graduate levels who want to gain theoretical grounding over the changing perspectives of the information science and the profession witnesses in last decades.

ROADMAP OF THE CONTENT

Overall we have adopted a simple style of writing that has been carefully maintained as far the realm of possibility in the book. The book is divided into ten chapters.

Chapter 1 introduces the readers to the fundamental concepts of data, information and knowledge. The chapter also explores the affinity between data, information, knowledge, wisdom and understanding. It also explores the various proposition surrounding data, information and knowledge that view it as a part of sequential order. The focus of this chapter is to provide conceptual grounding of knowledge in particular.

Chapter 2 concentrates on the aspects of information communication. The goal of this chapter is to help the readers to gain an initial insight into various means, forms, barriers and models of communication of information

The purpose of Chapter 3 is to delve into larger aspect of information phenomena. It puts forth the heavily contested various approaches surrounding the information phenomena. It explores the variant typologies, nature and usages of information. Lastly it describes in detail the various vehicles to represent information.

Chapter 4 gives an overview of Information Science, its genesis, various forms, methods and the interdisciplinary nature. It also describes the interdisciplinary nature of information science with various disciplines.

Chapter 5 focuses on metrics issues of information productivity. The manner in which the information is being generated there is an urgent need to quantify the various facets of information. It provides an introduction to the concept of Bibliometrics, Scientometrics, Webometrics, Cybermetrics and Informetrics. This effort has different mechanics that concentrates on various tools and mechanisms to carry information productivity metrics studies.

Chapter 6 looks specifically at the concept of information systems and system theories. This chapter centers on the various management support systems: Management Information Systems, Decision Support Systems and the Expert System. It addresses the fundamental theoretical issues of information systems like functions, types, characteristics, architecture etc.

Chapter 7 covers salient issues surrounding the emanating information society and their repercussions. It stresses on the factors that shaped the information society. Historical, Political and Economic perspectives have been discussed. With the upsurge in information productivity there has been realization of information as motor to economic pursuits. It also provides an overview of information industries and the emerging information profession.

The continuous expansion of e-resources availability and digitized materials has landed people into sea of information. Information tributaries enriched through new media and technologies has made the information sea much deeper. People feel submerged into this sea while seeking information. Chapter 8 is a discussion of prominent Web-resources that are productive information sources.

Chapter 9 looks at the emerging need of information literacy to avoid information fog and ensure higher satisfaction of the library users. It discusses in detail the need, goals, specifications, models and various methods of information literacy. With the sharp changes from library science to information science there is larger emphasis on information as well as content at right time.

Chapter 10 concludes the book with the brief discussion of Knowledge management and its implications in libraries. It surmises the key issues and the criticality of managing knowledge in the information profession.

We would like to acknowledge with thanks the work of

authors that we have incorporated to justify our discussion. We would also like to extend our thanks to professionals and students who gave consistent feedback and support to complete this conceptual endeavour.

Authors

1

Data, Information and Knowledge

"Whoever undertakes to set himself up as a judge of truth and knowledge is shipwrecked by the laughter of the gods."

- Albert Einstein

It is general disposition to use the words 'data', 'information' and 'knowledge' identically. Although these words are mutually related yet knowledge is not information and information is not data. A candid assessment is requisite to understand their connotation.

The word data is derived from Latin word 'datum' which means anything that is given. Data is a prerequisite to information that metamorphoses into knowledge. Data is a raw material from which information is extracted. It is bits of information that serves informative purpose. It is a representation of characters set that has no meaning on its own. In other words data merely constitute bare symbols, fact, figure, and idea. After processing meaning is attached with data that becomes information. It can be best understood with an example. The digits 221005 have no meaning as such. But if we are told that it is the pin code of Varanasi it becomes information. Processed in other way it can be a telephone number or date of birth of an individual.

International encyclopedia of information and library

science (Routledge, 2003) defines data as general term for quantitative or numerically encoded information.

Information is the sum total of processed data. Information is always propelled by some meaning and purpose. Defining information has led to contestation of multifarious opinions that has been dealt in the other section of the book.

Knowledge is the understanding of a subject matter acquired through proper study and experience. It is said to be a state of awareness beyond understanding.

According to Russell Ackoff, the content of the human mind can be classified into five categories:

1. **Data**: symbols
2. **Information**: data that are processed to be useful; provides answers to "who", "what", "where", and "when" questions
3. **Knowledge**: application of data and information; answers "how" questions
4. **Understanding**: appreciation of "why"
5. **Wisdom**: evaluated understanding.

Ackoff presumes that the first four categories relate to the past; they deal with what has been or what is known. Only the fifth category, wisdom, deals with the future because it incorporates vision and design. With wisdom, people can create the future rather than just grasp the present and past. But achieving wisdom isn't easy; people must move successively through the other categories.

Gene Bellinger, Durval Castro, Anthony Mills in Data, Information, Knowledge and Wisdom *(http://www.systems-thinking.org/dikw/dikw.htm)* have shown the transition from data, to information, to knowledge, and finally to wisdom

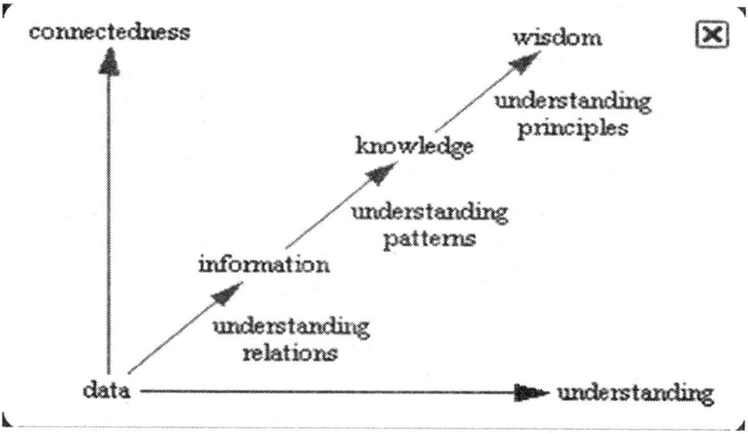

Scholars have also left no stone unturned to validate the differences between data, information and knowledge.

Sharon Daniel in The Database: an aesthetics of dignity has opined that it is people and computers who collect data and impose patterns on it. These patterns are seen as information which can be used to enhance knowledge. These patterns can be interpreted as truth, and are authorized as aesthetic and ethical criteria. Events that leave behind perceivable physical or virtual remains can be traced back through data. Marks are no longer considered data once the link between the mark and observation is broken.

On the other hand, M.M. Kashyap in Data processing and computer application in library. J.Lib.Inf.Sci. 7(1) Jun 1982:62-63 views information as the knowledge obtained by processing the data or the meaning derived from data.

R.G. Prasher in Information and its Communication (Medallion, 2003) has argued that data is a set of constituents of information which may or may not convey any logical meaning. When this data is processed , organized and relationship among data is established facilitating proper comprehension of the issue, it yields information.

Contrary to the above arguments, Beynon-Davies uses the concept of a sign to distinguish between data and information. He argues that data are symbols while information occurs when symbols are used to refer to something.

According to Alex and David Benet, Organizational survival in the new world», Butterworth-Heinemann, (US, 2004) 'a bite (of information) should be taken, chewed, digested, and acted upon so that it becomes knowledge'

RELATIONSHIP BETWEEN DATA, INFORMATION & KNOWLEDGE

Various authors have attempted to highlight the differences between data, information, knowledge and wisdom through a hierarchy. Some of the hierarchical structures has been mentioned below:

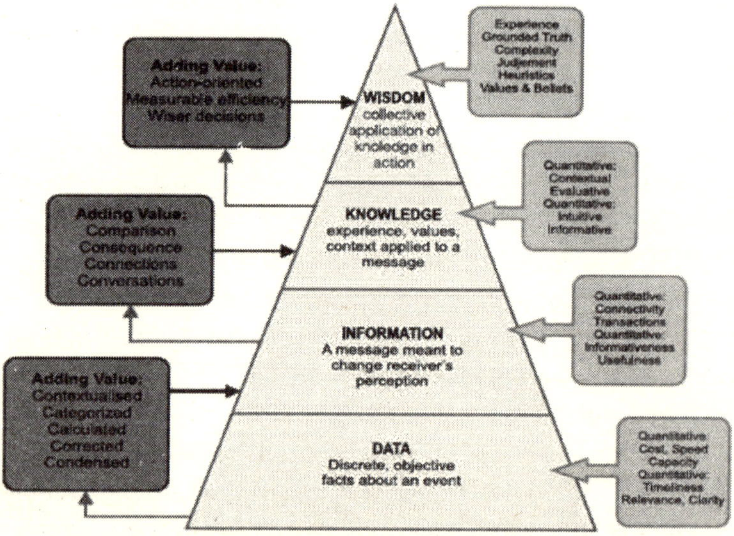

(*http://www.trainmor-knowmore.eu/FBC5DDB3.en.aspx*)

Source: Adapted from Liebowitz, (2003)

Data is an essential ingredient to information. Different types of data yield different meanings. When the data is brought in the purview of awareness it becomes information. By collecting information we make certain generalization that matures to knowledge. The accumulated knowledge over a period of time blossoms into a state of an ability to think and act wisely utilizing knowledge, experience, understanding, common sense and insight called wisdom.

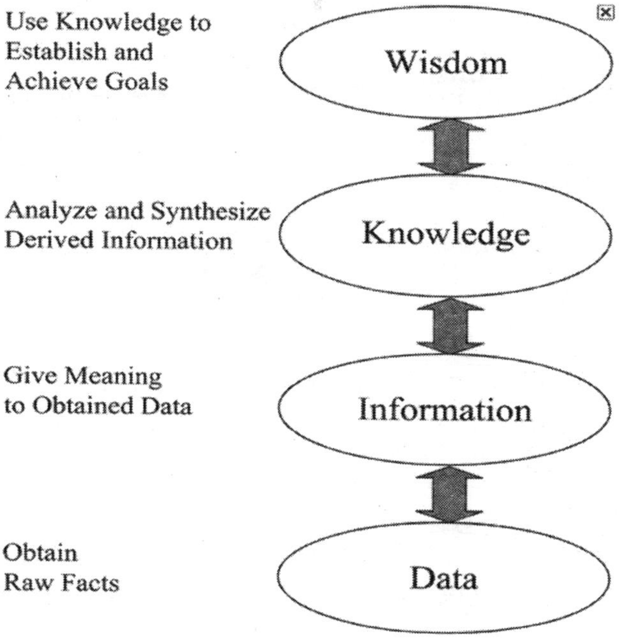

http://www.emeraldinsight.com/journals.htm?articleid=1411088&show=html

KNOWLEDGE

Information organized and evaluated in the human mind to use it purposefully is knowledge. The term is used parallel to understanding. However, different people have different understanding on knowledge. Some of the important opinions put forth by the scholar are:

- Knowledge implies total knowledge acquired by man during his lifetime.

- What we know, what we understand or what we are familiar with is knowledge
- Knowledge is the acquaintance, familiarity or understanding about anything or something.
- Knowledge is nothing but the state or fact of knowing
- Social interaction among each other yields a new knowledge
- Knowledge is the sum total of ideas conserved by human civilization
- Knowledge is an agglomeration of universe of ideas
- Knowledge is the process of acquiring something new
- Universe of knowledge focuses on universe of documents and universe of readers
- Knowledge is the sum total of ideas acquired by man through ages
- Knowledge is related to some ideas that a person acquires as a result of his interaction with certain entities
- Knowledge is familiarity or understanding of a phenomenon
- Knowledge emerges as a result of interaction between knowee and the knower
- Knowledge is the conscious expertise felt through the sensory organs
- Accumulation of ideas leads to knowledge

Characteristics

- Infinite
- Continuum
- Dynamic nature
- Cumulative

Orders of knowledge

According to Bliss there are three orders of knowledge:

1. Developmental order : In this order knowledge evolves out which is generated by various institutions, societies and cultures.

2. Pedagogic order : In this order knowledge is taught to young students and children

3. Pragmatic order : It implies the implication and utilization of knowledge to solve problems in hand.

Types of knowledge

Knowledge can be categorized in various ways on different ways:

I. On the basis of accessibility

- *Public knowledge* : Knowledge readily accessible to public.
- *Private knowledge* : Knowledge held by a person or an individual. Everybody does not have access to this knowledge
- *Procedural knowledge* : Knowledge gained through procedures

II. On the basis of interaction

- *Priori knowledge* : Knowledge which does not require any kind of interaction with the world. e.g. All bachelors are unmarried
- *Posteriori knowledge* : It is the outcome of interaction with the world or surroundings. e.g. Some bachelors are very happy

III. On the basis of availability

- *Social knowledge* : Knowledge which is freely or easily accessible to common public is social knowledge.
- *Personal knowledge* : Knowledge which is held by a single person. They are confidential in nature.

IV. On the basis of subject

- *Rational knowledge* : It is based on certain logic or reasoning
- *Intuitive knowledge* : It is the outcome of thinking or a thought process
- *Scientific knowledge* : It is the outcome of scientific procedures

V. On the basis of codification

- *Tacit knowledge* : It is highly personal and hard to formalize, making it difficult to communicate or share with others.
- *Explicit knowledge* : It is formally codified and has been expressed properly.
- *Implicit knowledge* : This type of knowledge can be expressed but has not been expressed.

VI. On the basis of approach

- *Procedural knowledge* : It represents the understanding of how to carry out a specific procedure
- *Declarative knowledge* : It is shallow knowledge that can be readily recalled. It is conscious and routine knowledge that resides in short-term memory.
- *Semantic knowledge* : It is highly organized chunk of knowledge that resides in long-term memory.
- *Episodic knowledge* : It represents the knowledge based on episodes or experimental information. Each episode is usually chunked in long-term memory

A block diagram representing the various types of knowledge has been plotted below:

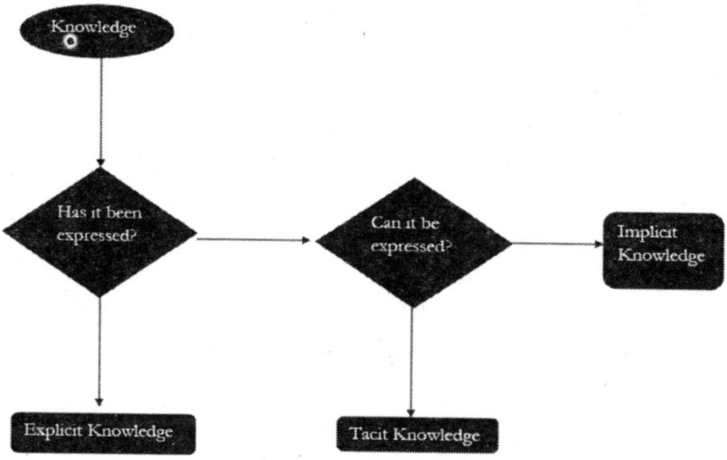

Tacit knowledge and explicit knowledge are not totally separate but mutually complementary entities. They interact with and interchange into each other in the creative activities of human beings.

There are four modes of knowledge conversion and they can be modeled as follows:

	Tacit knowledge *To*	Explicit knowledge
Tacit Knowledge	**Socialization**	**Externalization**
From		
Explicit Knowledge	**Internalization**	**Combination**

(*Source*: Knowledge conversion model as given by Hirotka Takeuchi and Ikujiro Nonaka in The knowledge creating company)

Modes of Knowledge Conversion

1. Socialization : (From tacit to tacit) : Socialization is a process of sharing experiences and thereby creating tacit knowledge. For e.g. Apprentices work with their masters learn craftsmanship not through language but through observation, imitation and practice.

2. Externalization: (From tacit to explicit) : Externalization is the process of articulating tacit knowledge into explicit concepts. When we attempt to conceptualize an image, we express its essence mostly in language writing is an act of converting tacit knowledge into articulable knowledge.

3. Combination (From explicit to explicit) : Combination is a process of systemizing concepts into knowledge systems. This mode of knowledge conversion involves combining different bodies of explicit knowledge. This happens through documents, meetings, telephone conversations or through networks.

4. Internalization (From explicit to tacit) : Internalization is a process of embodying explicit knowledge into tacit knowledge. It is closely related to "learning by doing". It happens when the experience is internalized.

REFERENCES

1. Prasher, R.G. Information and its communication. New Delhi, Medallion Press, 1991, p.13
2. Brookes, B.C. Foundation of information science. J. Inf. Sci. 2 (3-4) 1980; 125-33, 209-21, 269-75; 3(1) 1981:3-12
3. Machulp, F. and Mansfield, U. Study of information, inter-disciplinary messages. N.Y, Wiley, 1983, 743p.
4. Ackoff, R. L., "From Data to Wisdom", Journal of Applies Systems Analysis, Volume 16, 1989 p 3-9. {http://www.systems-thinking.org/dikw/dikw.htm}
5. Kashyap, M.M.. Data processing and computer application in library. J.Lib.Inf.Sci. 7(1) Jun 1982:62-63
6. P. Beynon-Davies (2002). Information Systems: An introduction to informatics in organizations. Basingstoke, UK: Palgrave Macmillan. ISBN 0-333-96390-3.
7. P. Beynon-Davies (2009). Business information systems. Basingstoke, UK: Palgrave. ISBN 978-0-230-20368-6.
8. Alex and David Benet, Organizational survival in the new

world», Butterworth-Heinemann, (US, 2004)

9. Debons, A. Foundations of Information Science. In Information: An integrated view. Boston, Mass:G.K. Hall,1980

10. Rubin, Richard E. (2004) Foundations of library and information science. New York: Neal-Schuman

11. International Encyclopedia of Information and Library Science. (2003). London: Routledge

12. Encyclopedia of Library and Information Science (2010) New York: CRC Press

13. Rowley, J.E. and Turner, C.M.D. (1976) Dissemination of information. London:Andra

14. Chizm, R.M. (1977) The theory of knowledge. New Delhi: Prentics-Hall

15. Sharma, Pandey S.K. (1990) Universe of knowledge and research methodology. Delhi:Ken publications

2
Communication

"Think like a wise man but communicate in the language of the people"
— W.B. Yeats

The word communication is derived from a latin word 'communis' which means 'commonness' or to share or to participate. Communication is the prime mover of information. It is the process which enables the exchange of messages, meanings, facts, ideas, opinions or emotions with other people. It means to convey a message by one person to another so that another person may understand, follow and implement the message.

MEANS OF INFORMATION COMMUNICATION

Humanity is confronting with the broad effects of modern technology. The unintended consequence of the technological marvels has been the availability of multifarious channels for communication. The surging appetite for information communication in the last decades has been satisfied through these channels.

In a layman language communication can be understood as:

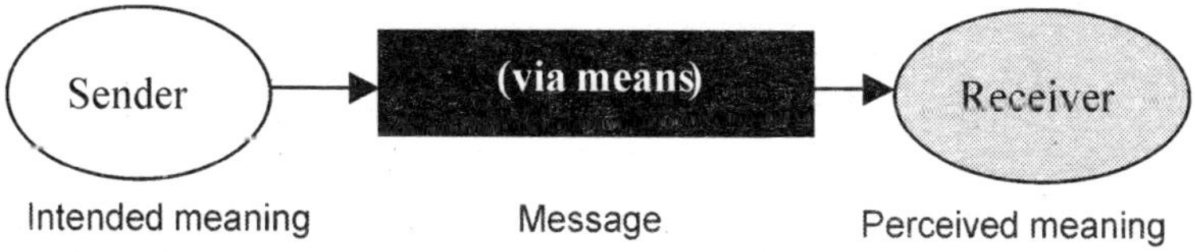

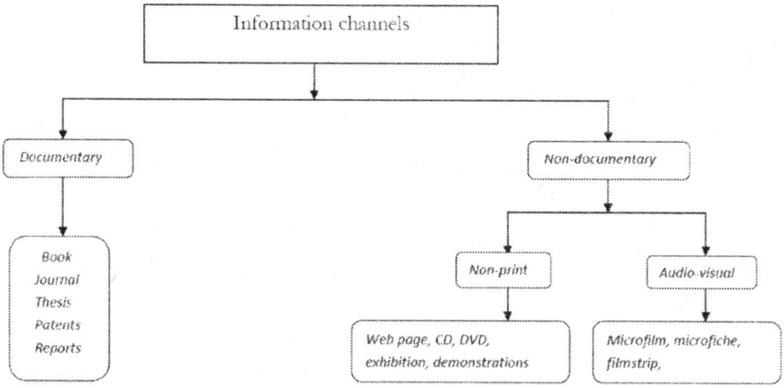

Parthasarthy has put forth two channels of communication:

1. Informal Channels

Informal channels are of stiffly conventional nature. They are not in accordance with any prescribed official manner.

Some of common informal channels are:

a. Invisible colleges
b. Professional societies
c. Research associations
d. Public or private research establishments
e. Private consultants
f. Technical specialists
g. Information intermediaries
h. Faculty members of universities or institutions

2. Formal Channels

These channels are in accordance with prescribed or customary forms. They ensure a formal authorization.

R.G. Prasher in Information and its communication (Medallion, 2003) has put forth various formal channels of communication, which include:

a. Authors

b. Libraries and information centres

c. Universities

d. Government

e. Learned societies and autonomous bodies

f. Industrial houses

g. Book trade

h. Manufacturers and traders brochure

i. Mass media- Pres, Radio, Television

FORMS OF INFORMATION COMMUNICATION

The forms of communication are:

a. One to one e.g. email, telephone communication

b. One to many e.g. classroom situation, speech

c. Many to many e.g. group discussion

According to R.G. Prasher in Information and its communication (Medallion, 2003) there six forms of communication:

a. One- way communication e.g. radio or television

b. Two-way communication e.g. text chatting

c. Non-verbal communication e.g. facial communication

d. Verbal communication. e.g. letter, reports

e. Informal communication

f. Formal communication

f.1. Downward communication

f.2. Upward communication

f.3. Horizontal communication

f.4. Diagonal communication

BARRIERS TO INFORMATION COMMUNICATION

Effective communication is achieved when the message sent is received by cent accuracy, which is a rare phenomenon. It is because of various hurdles or barriers in the communication process. The hindrances distort the messages and the communication becomes ineffective and incomplete. Some of the barriers are:

1. Physical barrier

Physical barriers are communication interferences that occur in the environment in which communication occurs. Some of the interferences are:

a. Noise

Sudden distracting noise drowns the quality of voice message.

b. Physical distance

When receiver is far away from the sender it is difficult to determine whether the receiver has received, understood, accepted and properly acted upon the message or not for an effective communication.

c. Information overload

Unrestricted flow may result in overloading of information .For example people getting too many emails may tend to ignore mails that should be answered. People respond to information overload by simply escaping from the task of information communication.

2. Semantic barrier

Semantic is the science of meaning, words seldom mean

the same thing to two persons. The sender and the receiver have to choose one meaning from among many. If both of them choose the same meaning the communication will be perfect. But people use either the same words in different ways or different words in the same way.

Hence, semantics may be a barrier to communication and it is not only the words but actions, implication and the entire situational contents that produce misunderstanding. Also, technical language may not be easily understood by the receiver which is also a barrier in communication process.

3. Organizational barrier

a. Status differences

Organizations often express hierarchical rank through a variety of symbols (titles, offices etc.). Such differences may distort communication. If the sender has a higher status than that of the receiver, then he has a tendency of not disclosing all the information to the receiver just to maintain his importance. On the other hand if the status of the sender is lower than that of the receiver he will have to transmit that information that can please the superior.

b. Organizational facilities

An organization needs to hold meetings, suggestion boxes, and complaint boxes for effective communication to increase information potency.

c. Choice of channel

Choice of channel is a prerequisite for an effective communication. For illiterate people using written communication is a failure. Similarly face to face communication as well as demonstrations is highly effective for sales person.

d. Organization policies

Some organization don't share the information to all which affects the communication

4. Psychological or Emotional Barrier

The importance of communication depends on the mindset of both sides. Different persons can apprehend the message differently that adversely affects the free flow of communication. Some of the psychological barriers are:

a. Listening

Many a times, people find are reluctant to accept the nascent information if it conflicts with their pre existing conception and perception. This rigid attitude of receiver is a barrier to information communication.

b. Psychological behavior

When a receiver is emotionally disturbed or not in a state to receive information then he may fail to communicate effectively leading to communication gap.

c. Emotional behavior

At times when the superior have an attitude of losing their temper then subordinates may develop an attitude to keep themselves away of the communication cycle.

5. Personal barriers

These factors connote the personal issues between the sender and the receiver.

a. Trust

If the source of information lacks a justifiable authority then information can lose its grounds on account of trust which is a big barrier.

b. Ability

Many people generally tend to keep themselves away

from communication process which prevents the free flow of messages making it a big barrier.

c. Attention

Sometimes the receiver may not be interested in the message of the sender which obstructs the communication process.

6. Financial barriers

Sometimes people can't communicate their ideas and opinions in lack of necessary funds. Many international seminars or learned societies demand fund to present their papers or publish their writings thus blocking the healthy flow of communication process.

7. Technological barriers.

Time and again, technological innovation has kicked loose plenty of options like SMS, MMS, email, voicemail etc which needs one to be acquainted with the technology. Failure of the knowhow of a technology is hurdle to efficient communication.

8. Communication barrier

Inadequate information can be misleading. Many a times out of confusion sender creates befuddle messages like "I will reach there at sharp 10:00 tomorrow" "I will have midday meal at your home" whose semantics is unclear. The receiver cannot figure out what sender means to say.

David G Schwartz in Integrating knowledge transfer and communication-mediated communication: categorizing barriers and possible responses has carved a structure to represent information transfer barriers:

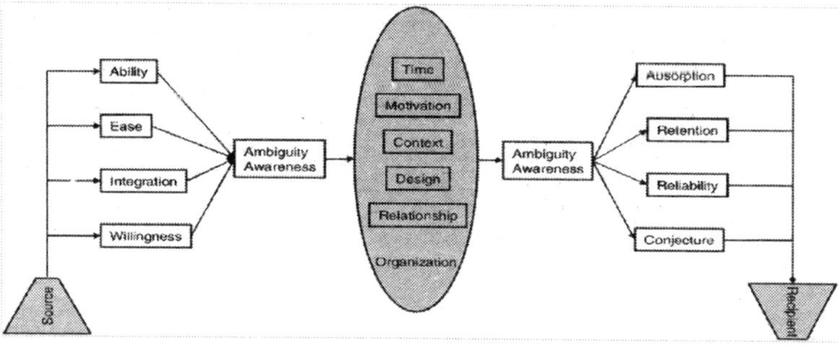

COMMUNICATION MODELS

It is like a fairytale to understand the phenomenon that is not visible. There are two good reasons for having models. The first is that models guide research process and serves as a means for academic discussion. The second reason is that models serve as a blue print to implement a conceptual framework.

C. David Mortensen in Communication: the study of human communication (New York: McGraw-Hill Book Co., 1972) has opined that a model is a systematic representation of an object or event in idealized and abstract form. Models are somewhat arbitrary by their nature. The act of abstracting eliminates certain details to focus on essential factors. The key to the usefulness of a model is the degree to which it conforms in point by point correspondence to the underlying determinants of communicative behavior. He further argues that communication models are merely pictures; they're even distorting pictures, because they stop or freeze an essentially dynamic interactive or transactive process into a static picture.

Communication models can be divided into four categories:

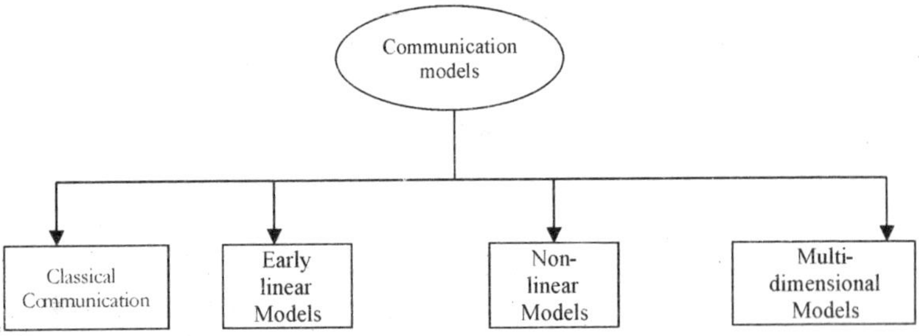

CLASSICAL COMMUNICATION MODELS

Classical communication model relates to the period of ascendancy of the ancient Greeks and Roman. The earliest communication model was put forth by the Greek philosopher Aristotle (384-322 B.C.)

- Aristotle's Model of Communication

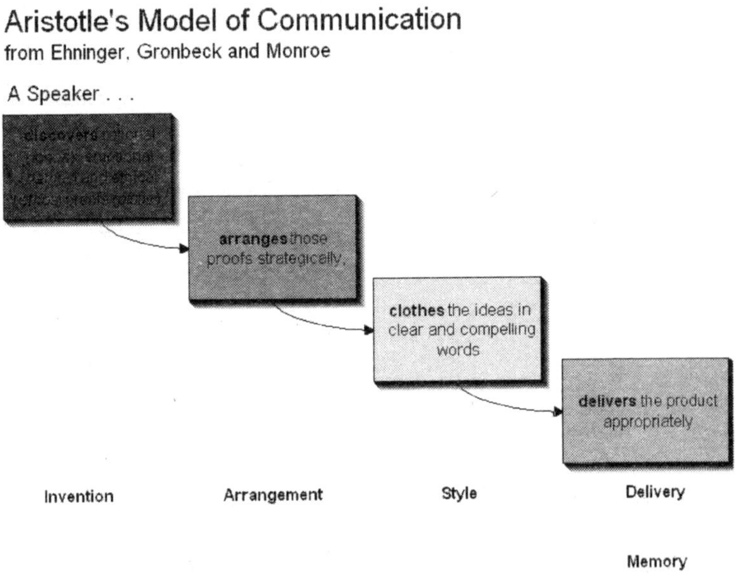

(*Source*: http://www.shkaminski.com/Classes/Handouts/Communication%20Models.htm)

According to Aristotle's model speaker has a pivotal role

in the communication process. He is the one responsible for entire communication process. Sender of the message drafts his thought content into a document which could disseminate his ideas to receiver. The success of an efficient and effective communication rests on the ability of the sender to generate, impress and influence the receivers. In a nutshell, speaker is the focal point of communication. Sender in the Aristotelian model of communication as a active communicator while the receiver is the passive one.

Following areas has to be kept in mind by the speaker (i.e. sender) of the message for a sound communication:

1. Selection of words
2. Better understandability of the targeted readers
3. Quality of the information content
4. Effective usage of language
5. Better communication skills
6. Ability to make an influence or heavily impact the users.

EARLY LINEAR MODELS

They relate or pertain to the characteristics of a work of art in which the workflow of the communication process is defined chiefly in terms of a linear measure. Models belonging to this typology are:

Shannon-Weaver Mathematical Model, 1949

Claude Shanon was a research scientist at Bell Telephone Company. He wanted to attain maximum telephone line capacity with minimal distortion. He put forth his mathematical theory of signal transmission exclusively for telephonic communications. But, Warren Weaver applied Shannon's concept of information loss to interpersonal communication.

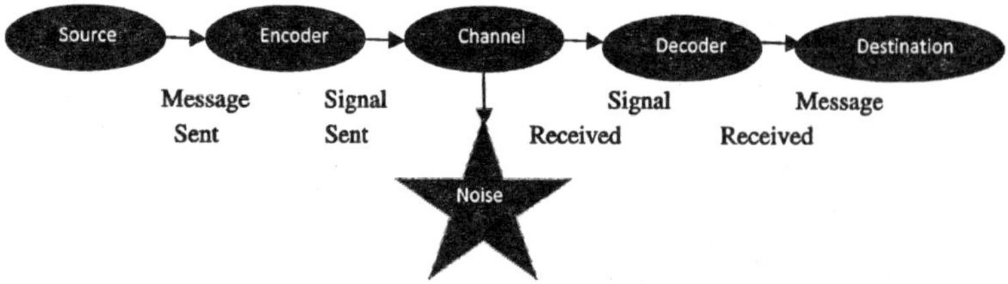

Elements of the model:

Source : It is the initiator, or origin, that starts the communication process. It may be an individual or a group who creates or generates the message.

Encoder : It receives the thought content generated by the sender and puts the same into suitable containers for interpretation and in a form which is easily assimilated by the user.

Message : Any idea, fact, raw data or information which is communicated from one end to the other end is message.

Channel : It is the medium through which any message (oral, written or digital) travels.

Noise : During the course of communication anything which hinders the free flow of information from the sender to the receiver is noise.

Decoder : It is the process of decoding or re-interpreting the message in a form that the intended receiver is able to understand.

Receiver : Receiver is the one who receives the sent out message.

Feedback : For an effective communication it is inevitable to know that whether the receiver has received the message understood it and acted properly.

A majority of concepts of this model are staples to the communication research:

1. *Entropy* : It is a measure of uncertainty in any system.
2. *Redundancy* : It is defined as the degree to which

information is not unique in the system.

3. *Noise* : It is the interference or distortion that hinders the healthy information flow blocking the reception of information.

4. Channel capacity: It is the measure of the maximal amount of information a channel can carry.

Berlo's S-M-C-R Model of Communication

This model is an adaptation of the Shannon-Weaver model developed by David Berlo in 1960.

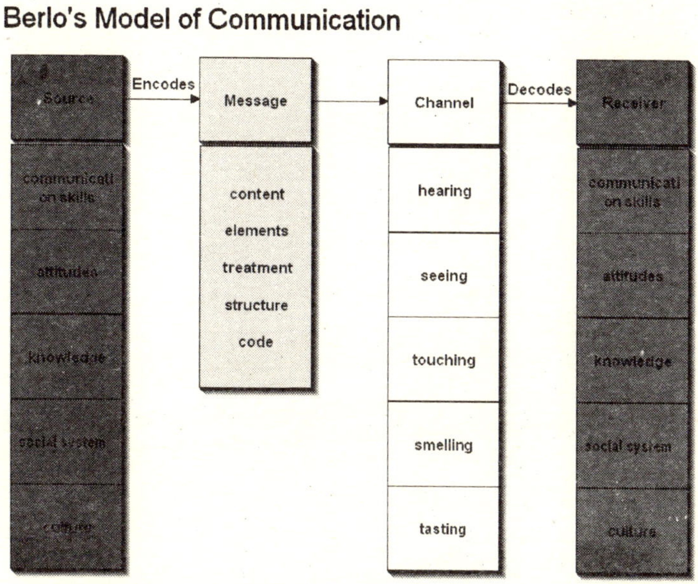

A Source encodes a message for a channel to a receiver who decodes the message: S-M-C-R Model.

NON LINEAR MODELS

They relate or pertain to the characteristics of a work of art in which the workflow of the communication process is defined chiefly in terms of a non-linear measure. Models belonging to this typology are:

Dance's Helical Spiral, 1967

According to this model communication is an ever-changing process and the way communication evolves from the generator to the receiver can be seen as a helical structure.

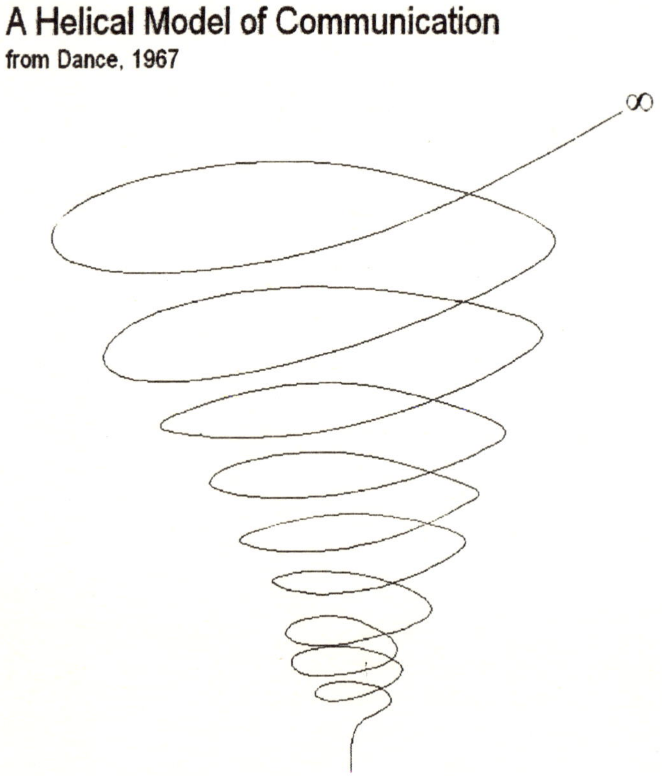

MULTI-DIMENSIONAL MODELS

Ruesch and Bateson Functional Model, 1951

They put forth four levels of communication process functioning simultaneously. At each level, four communicative functions: evaluating, sending, receiving and channeling takes place.

Level I Intrapersonal communication process

Level II Interpersonal communication process

Level III Communication between many people

Level IV Cultural level where large number of people are linked

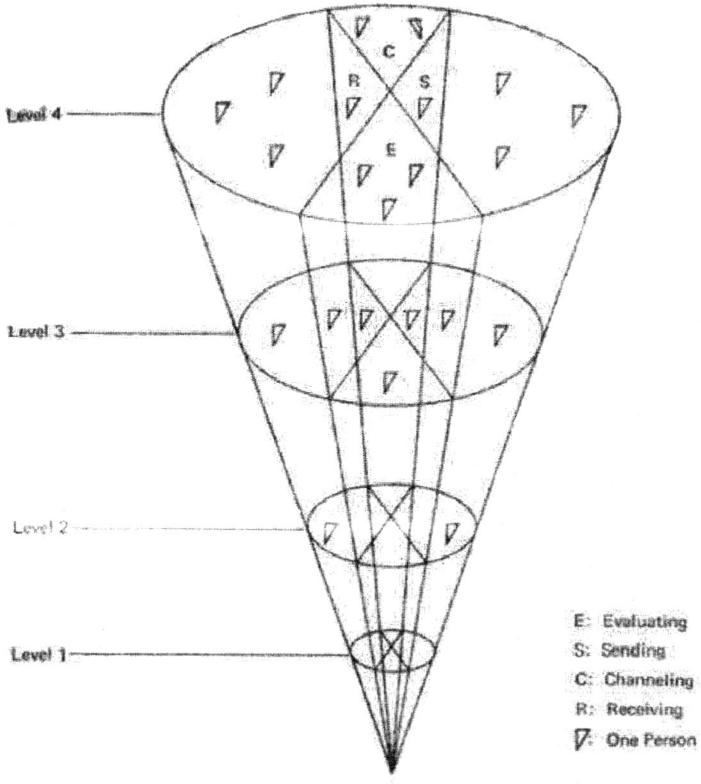

REFERENCES

1. Parthasarthy,S. Information communication barriers. In: National Conference on Scientific information for Defence, New Delhi, 25-26 Feb. 1936. Conference papers. New Delhi, DESIDOC, 1986, p.S5-1

2. R.G. Prasher in Information and its communication (Medallion, 2003)

3. David G Schwartz in Integrating knowledge transfer and communication-mediated communication: categorizing barriers and possible responses (http://www.palgravejournals.com/kmrp/journal/v5/n4/fig_tab/8500153f3.html)

4. C. David Mortensen in Communication: the study of human communication (New York: McGraw-Hill Book Co., 1972)

5. Rubin, Richard E. (2004) Foundations of library and information science. New York: Neal-Schuman

6. G.Bhattacharya in Information Sciences : a unified view through a system approach (IASLIC, 1978)

7. *Debons, A. Foundations of Information Science. In* Information: An integrated view. *Boston, Mass:GK. Hall,1980*

8. International Encyclopedia of Information and Library Science. (2003). London: Routledge

9. Encyclopedia of Library and Information Science (2010) New York: CRC Press

10. Rodriques, M.V. (2002) Effective Buisness communication. New Delhi: Concept.

11. Aggarwal, D.S. Lectures on universe of knowledge (1985) New Delhi: Academic Publications

12. Doyle, Lauren B. (1975) Information retrieval and processing. Los Angles: Melville Pub. Co

3
Information

"As a general rule, the most successful man in life is the man who has the best information." — **Benjamin Disraeli**

For the library and information professionals no value is more fundamental than a commitment to provide the people with information. Any message received and understood by intended audience is information. Although it sounds simple, yet people have put forth multitudes of opinions depending on their nature of study and research on information. There has yet not been any widely agreed definition or a sound theoretical base of information due to its intangibility. Defining any term seeks to study the qualitative and quantitative behavior. Information is an intangible product of human intellect which can neither be seen nor felt but can be only expressed. It has been a contested project to define information among the savants. It would be disingenuous labor to present a singular vision on the topic. In lack of agreement of interpretations it would be fair to put forth the definitions currently in play.

Broadly seven typologies of definition have been explicated:

a. Communicatory or Semiotic Approach

This approach attempts to depict the communicatory role

of information from one point to another. How the transfer of information from the source to recipient affect the status of the recipient.

Main pronouncers of this school of thought are Madden, Bateson, Brookes, Mackhlup, Nauta and Losee. Madden defines information as stimulus which expands or amends the world view of the informed. On the other hand, Bateson is of the opinion that information is a difference that makes a difference after understanding. While Brookes has put forward a fundamental equation showing the relationship between information and knowledge. He argues that knowledge structure in the mind is changed in some way with the input of information. Mathematically it is represented as-

$$K[S] + \Delta I = K[S + \Delta S]$$

Where, $K[S]$ = existing knowledge structure

$K[S + \Delta S]$ = modified information structure

ΔI = new information

ΔS = effect of modification to the existing knowledge

Fritze Mackhlup considers information as flow of messages involving the act of being told. Similarly, Whitemore and Yovits argues that information is data of value to decision making. Rowley surmises information as data that can be transmitted between individuals and each individual can use it accordingly. G.Bhattacharya opines that information is the message conveyed or intended to be conveyed by a systematized body of ideas, or its accepted or acceptable substitutes.

According to Nauta information is the meaning that is common to all the different ways of expressing the meaning. Further, Losee argues that information is produced by all processes and it is the values in the characteristics of the process. He says "information is always informative about something, being a component of the output or result of the process. This aboutness or representation is the result of a processes or function producing the representation of the input which might be output of another function and represents its input and so forth". He cites an example of the process of baking of cake. Cake provides information about both the process and original ingredients. The choice of high quality ingredients will affect the outcome. Varying the process such as the amount of time in the oven also changes the final product.

b. Activity based approach

In this approach attempts have been undertaken to define, information as an event put forth by Pratt which occurs at some unique point in time and space to some particular individual.

c. Propositional approach

This school of thought considers a piece of information to be claim of world or a proposition. Main contenders are Derr, Drestske, Fox.

Derr surmises that information is an abstract, meaningful representation of determinations which have been made of objects. Drestske opines that information is capable of yielding knowledge and since knowledge requires truth, information requires it also.

Fox put forth that information is collective proposition claim of a set of statements in a given context, provided the agent is in a position to know.

d. Structural approach

Thompson argues that information is a product that results from applying the process of organization to the raw material of experience. According to him data to the scientist are like colors on the palette of the painter. It is by the artistry of his theories that we are informed. It is the organization that is the information.

e. Social approach

Cornelius conceives that information should be seen as socially constructed within a set of practices. A practice is a coherent set of actions and beliefs which we conform to along with other people in our practice (profession or game) and it has its own internal logic and ethic. On the other hand, Gougen says an item of information is an interpretation of a configuration of signs for which members of some social groups are accountable.

f. Multitype information approach

According to Dervin information is external world (what information we seek), information is internal world(what information we already have). Information is the reconciliation between the two worlds. Bates concludes that information is pattern of organization of matter and energy

g. Deconstructing approach

Lastly, Frohmann attempts to replace the centrality of information as the focus of information studies and science studies with the centrality of practices surrounding documents.

TYPES OF INFORMATION

The intensive study and research on information in the last decades has started a new epoch seeking new awareness of information. People find it modish to deride earlier notions in light of novel ideas. As one senses a fatiguing fight of interpretations to define information, the fecund power of human brain has sprouted into various manifestations of information typologies.

On the basis of characteristics G.Bhattacharya in Information Sciences: a unified view through a system approach (IASLIC, 1978) has spotted two universally accepted varieties of information viz.

1. Discursive information; and

2. Non-discursive information

Discursive information *is the message conveyed by a systematized body of ideas or its accepted or acceptable substitutes, having one or many of the following attributes relating to its treatment and/or expression:*

- Ranging over a wide field;
- Proceeding logically or coherently from topic to topic;
- Proceeding from logical abstraction to logical interpretation.

For example, the set of ideas conveyed by defining information science is discursive information.

The organized bodies of idea taking the shape of statement that conveys information consisting of unit fact and does not show any attributes of discursive information are non-discursive information.

For example, if one asks 'What is your religion?' One can say 'I am Hindu' or 'Hindu'. It consists of unit fact and does not show any attributes of discursive information. Henceforth it is non-discursive information.

Non-discursive information is further divided into two groups:

a. Qualitative information

Qualitative non-discursive information describes unit facts in relation to quality.

b. Quantitative information

Quantitative non-discursive information describes unit facts in relation to quantity.

J.H. Shera *in Foundation of education for librarianship has segregated information into six types:*

1. Conceptual information : It refers to the formulation of mental conception of bare ideas and thoughts about any problem.

2. Empirical information : Information derived from or guided by experience or relating to experiment and observation rather than theory is said to be empirical information. They are verifiable by experience or experiment.

3. Procedural information : Information providing a well established method of acting or progressing in a course of action is known as procedural information.

4. Stimulatory information : These informations are stimulated by existing theories.

5. Policy information : It provides a plan or definite course of action for the sake of expediency or facility to be pursued by an individual, government, party, business etc. It is an indispensable tool for decision making.

6. Directive information : It gives an authoritative instruction or direction for proper coordination work between team work or group activity.

On the basis of nature of production of information Moraine Valley Community College Library/Learning Resources Center have categorized information as:

1. Scholarly information : They report the advancements, new findings or ideas in a field in to quench the quest of information. They are available in books, articles in scholarly journals and websites.

2. Professional / Trade information : They inform, promote and usually strengthen the trade market or learned societies. They are available to the people in the form of trade magazines, journals and association websites.

3. Government information : They are an aid to inform the policies or programme of the government to the common people or the decision makers. They are commonly available as printed government publications or official government publications.

4. Information providing facts, definition or statistics: These information presents facts, definitions or statistics with little explanation or evaluation. They can be obtained from books and websites.

5. Information providing overviews : They provide overview or background on a subject. They can be found out from encyclopedias, dictionaries, other books and websites.

6. Information providing news or current events : They report daily events in a scheduled manner across the nation or worldwide. They are available as newspapers, newsmagazines, and news websites.

7. Information providing opinions : They contain the ideological thoughts put forth by anyone. It depends upon the reader to justify the credibility of the author and he may or may not follow him.

8. Uncredited information : They provide information on personal interests. No one is accountable of the thought content of the information. They are available in the form of personal websites and blogs.

According to Kathy Tyner, there are five types of information: facts, concepts, procedures, processes and principles.

Fact: It is a bit of information that identifies an object, person, place or data.

For example : 14.08.1947. If you recall the fact then you know that is the date when got freedom.

Concept: It is a group of items or ideas that share common features.

For example: If you see cat and tiger you recall the concept that you have and distinguish between cat and tiger by their features.

Procedure: It provides a series of steps to prepare or do something.

For example, while preparing tea you recall the procedures and prepare tea.

Process: It describes how anything works or operates.

Principles: They are certain rules well established guidelines that predict an outcome.

Lastly, on the basis of communication or pattern of Shannon weaver model of information transfer information can be further divided as:

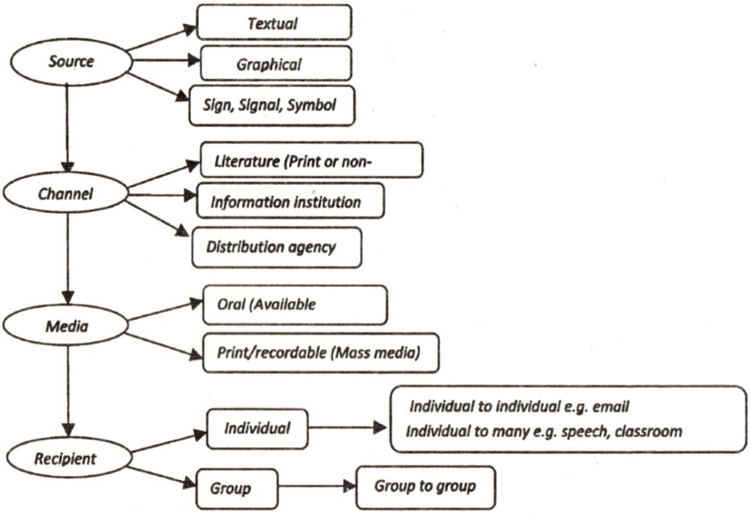

Voigt has also put forth four categories of information. These are:

1. Current : It is a type of information belonging to the time actually in progress or of the immediate present.

2. Everyday : It is a form of information pertaining to everyday occurrence.

3. Catching up : It is a form of information that one comprehends with the intellect. It has a tendency to grasp eagerly to update oneself.

4. Exhaustive : It seeks to provide comprehensive or exhaustive information on a subject or a topic.

NATURE OF INFORMATION

1. Information is piecemeal, fragmented that changes according to context.
2. Information is inevitable for an organization in decision making or feasibility studies.
3. Information is sharable, expandable and compressible.
4. Information is timely and ephemeral.
5. Information cannot be represented quantitatively.
6. Information requires structure or context for its representation.
7. The importance of information varies from person to person.
8. Information is a democratic resource.
9. Information is an element of knowledge spectrum.
10. Information requires special measures like copyright or IPR to prevent plagiarism.
11. Information becomes obsolete with time.
12. Information is universal in nature.
13. Information has interdisciplinary application.
14. Information is heterogeneous.

Rathswol states that the nature of information is taken in terms of four components:

a. Commodity : It represents empirical content of communication and knowledge.

E.g. Some events, some state of world.

b. Process : It connotes structural and original aspect of communication and knowledge. Information as an process is represented as something.

E.g. generic structure.

c. State of knowing : Information as a state of knowing relates directly to the structural-functional aspects of human knowing activity. It is representative of the effect of information in terms of changes in a human knower.

d. Environment : The concept of environment refers to man-machine, man-man system etc. command & control system within which certain data-information transformation occurs.

USAGES OF INFORMATION

1. Tool in science and technology.
2. Decision making in business transactions.
3. Societal development.
4. Sales promotion.
5. Better financial management.
6. Training
7. Tool for marketing of products and services.
8. To quench information demand.
9. Technology transfer.
10. In industry as:
    - Identification of product
    - Market & Marketing
    - Manufacture technology
    - Equipment & machines
    - Standardization
    - Administration & management
    - Planning

INFORMATION AS A RESOURCE / COMMODITY

Several scholars are of the opinion that information is a gem and key to all developments. As a resource it has a pivotal role to play in the societal development. Access to right information at a right time can open new doors for furthering study and advanced research. We are living in a scientific era where all our old beliefs and thoughts are dead and science is our salvation. It would not have been possible without the fecund power of human intellect playing parasitic role on information.

People need information on different areas in different forms having different thrust areas and explanation penetration. Scholars, scientists, lawyers, politicians attend programmes, meetings, conferences to metamorphose their information bank to keep themselves updated. This inevitable attitude of information has opened a Pandora box of information attributes. Information has been referred as 'power' 'vital' 'commodity' 'resource' and much more. All the resources depend on information. For example, wind energy cannot be harvested without the information of weather conditions.

Henceforth, people have started depending on information knowhow for their subsistence. This dependency has been judiciously exploited for commercial motives by corporate bodies. It has become an essential resource or commodity for the people. New branches like information economics, information industry have also come into light.

INFORMATION FORAGING THEORY

It includes the ways to find out a flawless path of reaching the information goals of users during searching. It suggests that the way human seek information is not unlike the way wild animals gather food (Pirolli, 2007; Pirolli and Card, 1999). The theory constitutes three models:

Information Scent Model

Information Scent Model demonstrates how people catch sight of available information resources from the existing pool of information resources.

Information Diet Model

Information Diet Model elucidates a set of strategies deployed in sorting and absorbing a piece of information.

Information Patch Model

Information Patch Model points out the strategy and decision taking in the chase for another information resource

INFORMATION TRANSFER CYCLE

Information transfer cycle refers to the process of creation, collection, storage, dissemination and retrieval of information. It refers to how information is transferred to the users from its sources.

Beth M. Shephard in A forum of electronic journals: change, challenge, opportunity has put forth the processes of information transfer cycle:

1. Creation of material (authorship, publication)
2. Dissemination (marketing, sales)
3. Organization (indexing, cataloguing)
4. Diffusion (Availability to users)
5. Utilization (By readers/ researchers)

Steps of Information Transfer

S.No	Methods	Activity	Key Players
1.	Generation of information	In this process information is generated for a targeted user group	Authors Editors Institutions
2.	Collection or gathering of information	In this process the generated information is gathered and organized	Scientists Publishers Institutional archives Online publishing
3.	Storage of information	In this process information is stored at any place.	Libraries Documentation centres Information centres Databases Databanks

			Repositories Information networks
4.	Dissemination of information	In this process the generated information is disseminated to the intended readers through proper containers.	Books Periodicals Oral diffusion Reprography Translation CAS SDI Reference service Indexing Abstracting

REPRESENTATION OF INFORMATION

Representation of information is the act or instance of portraying a mental imagery of some term, character or idea. Information is nebulous, unformed, unshaped and nondescript entity that is beyond mental conceptualization. In order to clasp the essence of information, it needs to be configured, ordered, and structured.

Kevin McGarry in The changing context of information: an introductory analysis (LA, 1993) opines that information should have a discriminable attribute if it has to be perceived by the receiver which can distinguish it from the surrounding phenomena.

McGarry has identified three classes of vehicles for information carriage. These are:

- Signals
- Symbols
- Signs

SIGNALS

Anything that serves to indicate, warn, direct or command that can be through light or a gesture or an act is signal like a traffic signal, a signal to sit. They are an act or event that causes some action. Signal is an impulse response to a stimulus whose variations represent information.

According to Kevin McGarry in The changing context of information: an introductory analysis (LA, 1993) signal is a form of sign with an emphasis on the need for some form of action to follow and requiring some form of response from the receiver.

Characteristics of signals

1. Signals are dynamic in nature. They change with time.
2. Signals are purely contextual.
3. The semantics of signal varies from person to person.
4. Signals are always responsive.
5. Signals relates to a particular society, and its ideas, customs and art.
6. Signals are transmittable.

Types of signals

a. Deterministic signal : Signals that can be pre determined before occurrence and can be easily predicted are known as deterministic signal.

Example : Weather signals

b. Random signal : Signals that can never be predicted and occurs randomly are known as random signals.

Example: Signals during medical tests

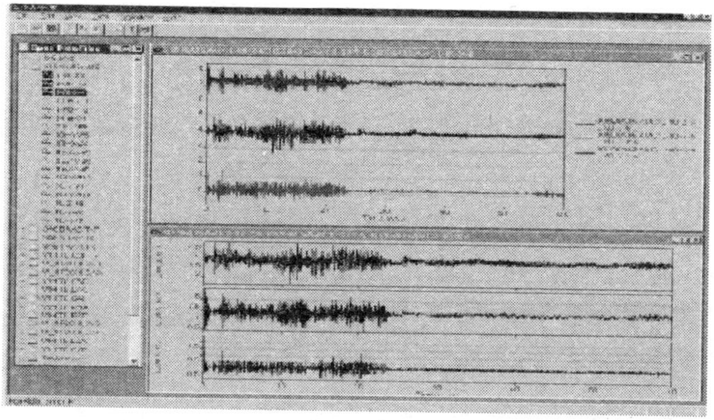

c. **Noise signals :** Generally noise is considered as barrier to information communication however, noise is also a signal that is unpleasant to our ears.

Example : vehicles horn

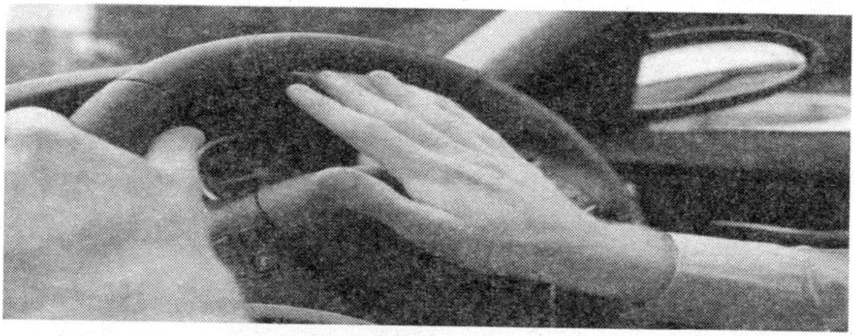

SYMBOLS

Symbols are figure or character or mark or a combination of letters that suggests something else to the unconscious mind. For example the chemical symbol Ag or a Red Cross symbol.

Wor. Bro. Clive Herron in The value of symbols (http://www.freemasons-freemasonry.com/herron1.html) has referred to symbols as "visual shorthand" that suggest abstract concepts.

Kevin McGarry in The changing context of information: an introductory analysis (LA, 1993) argues that symbols are a special kind of sign representing an object, idea or event that are intended to elicit the same kind of emotional response as if the things they referred to were immediately present.

Characteristics of Symbols

1. Symbols are static in nature.
2. Symbols to some extent are contextual.
3. Symbols are independent of situation.
4. Symbols are highly customizable and reusable.
5. Symbols are used to promote logo or symbol to influence consumers.
6. Symbols are independent of culture

Types of Symbols

a. Abstract symbols : They are non-representational in nature where the concrete realities or actual instances are difficult to figure it out which connote an abstract idea.

Example:

b. Living symbols : They portray a living body as a symbol. It has flair of life in it.

Example:

c. Animated symbols : It is the random display of image in a sequence to create an illusion of movement.

Example :

d. Compound symbols : It is the amalgamation of text, graphics as well as animated images to present a combined effect of a symbol.

Example:

e. Artifacts symbols : Artifacts symbols represent man-made materials or human artifacts around us.

Example :

f. Astrological symbols : It consists of zodiac as well as heavenly bodies which are potrayed as a symbol for astrological and astronomical calculations. They are basically abstract in nature whose semantics is unclear.

Example:

g. Text symbols : It is the representation of written language where plain texts are used to represent a symbol.

Example :

BULLS

SIGNS

Signs are arbitrary mark, figure or symbol used for representation. Wikipedia defines sign as an entity which signifies another entity. The way in which a sign signifies is a topic in semiotics and philosophy of language.

On the other hand, Kevin McGarry in The changing context of information: an introductory analysis (LA, 1993) concludes that sign is a physical evidence of the thing or event it represents. For example, smoke is a sign of fire but one can't be sure whether the smoke is due to fire or burning of charcoal or something else. One can't be sure till he does not conform it personally.

Sign comprises of three components

Representation (Sign interpreter) : It includes the sign which is interpreted by the intended person.

Semiotic object : It is the object regarding which the sign is given. It connotes the semantics of the sign used.

Percipient (Sign perceiver) : It includes the receiver of the intended sign.

Characteristics of signs:

1. Signs can't be confirmed.
2. Signs are used to represent information beyond any cultural limitation.
3. Signs are always contextual.
4. Signs are a tool to start the preliminary phase of investigations.
5. Signs can be misleading, hence needs to be confirmed.
6. Signs are uncertain in nature.

Types of Signs

According to Peirce's theory of signs three are three typologies of signs:

1. According to Sign's own phenomenological category *(1903, 1904)*
    - *Qualisign*: It consists of quality of feeling.
    - *Sinsign* : It consists of an action or resistence or an actual occurrence of a fact.

- *Legisign* : It consists of a idea, a norm, a law or a habit.

2. According to phenomenological category of denoting object. *(1867)*
   - *Icon*: It is a sign that represents an object by ethicalness of its quality.
   - *Index*: It represents objects by quality of an actual connection involving them.
   - *Symbol* : It represents those objects which can be easily interpreted.

3- According to interpreter's way of denoting the object. *(1902, 1903)*
   - *Rheme* : It represents the objects in respect of quality.
   - *Dicisign* : It represents object in terms of its actual existence.
   - *Argument* : It represents object in light of law or habit.

REFERENCES

1. Madden,A.D. A definition of information J.Doc2004,60(1),9-23
2. Bateson,Gregory Steps to an ecology of mind Ballantine Books:New York,1972
3. Brookes,B.C. The foundation of information science J.ISc 1980,2(3-4),125-133
4. G.Bhattacharya in Information Sciences : a unified view through a system approach (IASLIC, 1978)
5. Nauta,Doedi The meaning of information Mounton:The Hague,1972
6. Losee,Robert A discipline independent definition of information science J.ISc 1997,48(3), 254-269
7. Pratt,Allan The information of the image: a model of the communication process Libri 1977,27(3),204-220,
8. Derr,Richard The concept of information in ordinary discourse Information process management 1985,21(6),489-499
9. Drestske,Fred Knowledge and the flow of information Cambridge :MIT Press, ,1981

10. Fox,Christopher Information and misinformation: an investigation of the notions of information, misinformation, informing and misinforming Greenwood Press

11. Thompson,Frederick The organization is information Am. Doc. 1968,19(3),305-308

12. Cornelius,Ian Information and interpretation

13. Gougen,Joseph Towards a social ethical theory of information

14. Dervin,Branda Useful theory of librarianship: communication not information

15. Frohmann,Bernd Deflating information

16. Bates,Marica J. Fundamental form of information

17. Moraine Valley Community College Library/Learning Resources Center (http://www.morainevalley.edu/library/handouts/types_of_information_0705.pdf)

18. (http://www.etc.edu.cn/eet/eet/articles/Infotypes/start.htm) Kathy Tyner , M.S.

19. Beth M. Shephard in A forum of electronic journals: change, challenge, opportunity

20. McGarry, Kevin The changing context of information: an introductory analysis (LA, 1993)

21. Tyner, Kathy M.S. Infotypes (http://www.etc.edu.cn/eet/eet/articles/Infotypes/start.htm.) Accessed on 15 Jan 2012.

22. Debons, A. Foundations of Information Science. In Information: An integrated view. Boston, Mass:G.K. Hall,1980

23. International Encyclopaedia of Information and Library Science. (2003). London: Routledge

24. Encyclopaedia of Library and Information Science (2010) New York: CRC Press

25. Mansfield, Una The wider scope of information research, (Current trends in information: research and theory, Bill Katz and Robin Kinder eds.) New York: Haworth, 1987,p.64

26. Pirolli, P. (2007)Information Foraging Theory: adaptive interaction with information, Oxford University Press.

27. Pirolli, P. and Card, S.K. (1999) Information Foraging, Psychological Review, 106, pp. 643-675

28. Sign (http://en.wikipedia.org/wiki/Sign) Accessed on 16 Jan, 2012

29. Peirce, C.S. (1897), "The Logic of Relatives", The Monist, v. VII, pp. 161-217. Reprinted in CP 3.456-552.

30. Peirce, C.S. (c.1902 MSS), "Minute Logic", CP 2.1-118.

31. Peirce, C.S. (c.1902 MS), "Reason's Rules"

32. Peirce, C.S. (1867), On a New List of Categories, Proceedings of the American Academy of Arts and Sciences 7 (1868), 287–298. Presented, 14 May 1867. Reprinted (Collected Papers (CP), v. 1, paragraphs 545–559), (Writings of Charles S. Peirce: A Chronological Edition, v. 2, pp. 49–59), (The Essential Peirce (EP) v. 1, 1–10).

33. Peirce, C.S. (c.1894 MS), What Is a Sign? Published in part in CP 2.281, 285, and 297-302, and in full in EP 2:4-10. Peirce Edition Project

34. Peirce, C.S. (1895 MS), Of Reasoning in General. Published in part in CP 2.282, 286-91, 295-96, 435-44, and 7.555-8, and in full in EP 2:11-26.

35. Peirce, C.S. (1867), Upon Logical Comprehension and Extension, Proceedings of the American Academy of Arts and Sciences, pp. 416-432. Presented 13 November 1867. Reprinted CP 2.391-426, Writings v. 2, pp. 70–86.

36. Peirce, C.S. (1896), The Regenerated Logic, The Monist, v. VII, n. 1, pp. 19-40, The Open Court Publishing Co., Chicago, Illinois, 1896, for the Hegeler Institute. Reprinted (CP 3.425-455). Internet Archive The Monist 7, p. 19.

37. Peirce, C.S. (c.1903 MS), Logical Tracts, No. 2, CP 4.418–509.

38. Peirce, C.S. (1904 Oct 12), A Letter to Lady Welby, CP 8.327–41.

39. Peirce, C.S. A Syllabus of Certain Topics of Logic, EP 2:
    - Peirce, C.S. (1903) Sundry Logical Conceptions, EP 2:267-88.
    - Peirce, C.S. (1903) Nomenclature and Divisions of Triadic Relations, as Far as They Are Determined, EP 2:289-99
    - Peirce, C.S. (1904 MS) New Elements (Kaina Stoicheia), pp. 235–63 in Carolyn Eisele, ed, The New Elements of Mathematics by Charles S. Peirce, Volume 4, Mathematical Philosophy. Reprinted (EP 2:300-24).

4

Information Science

"In science the credit goes to the man who convinces the world, not the man to whom the idea first occurs".

— Sir Francis Darwin

Information Science owes its genesis to a scientific background. Debates about the nature of information science, the scope of the discipline and its relations to other academic and professional areas are as old as the discipline itself. These are not merely navel-gazing, or arguments about terminology. They relate to the validity and viability of the discipline and have significance for the extent to which its unique contributions are recognized. It is a scientific approach relating to gathering, manipulation, classification, storage and dissemination of the recorded knowledge. Moreover, it is interdisciplinary in nature. Its development and scope cannot be confined to a single discipline. Although it is a science yet the word science does not connote to the subject rather a process that deals with character and usage of information. According to International encyclopedia of information and library science (Routledge, 2003) the dominance of scientific information in the information science was a demand-led phenomenon, determined by economics. Despite its origins, information science is a social science because it deals with an artifact of main information.

Information science first became known as a discipline during the 1950s. The first usage of the term in a paper by Farradane (1955:76), The discipline grew out of the longer-standing documentation movement, under numerous social, economic and technical influences. It is clear that, from the origins of the terms, there has been little agreement about the nature of information science, and indeed information scientists (Shapiro 1995, Bawden 2008, Robinson 2009).

Was the concern with the information of science, i.e., the practicalities of the handling of scientific and technical information, or with the science of information, i.e., the academic study of information phenomena? This question has never really been settled; in essence, it is the question of whether information science is a discipline, or a practical art.

Apparently, there is not a uniform conception of information science. The field seems to follow different approaches and traditions: for example,

i) objective approaches versus cognitive approaches, and

ii) the library tradition versus the documentation tradition versus the computation tradition.

The concept has different meanings, which imply different knowledge domains. Different knowledge domains imply different fields. Nevertheless, all of them are represented by the same name, information science. No wonder that scholars, practitioners and students are confused. (Zins 2007: 335)

It is fruitless travail to unravel the debate over nature and definition of information science. The profundity of sphere of study in information science is noteworthy. The multitudinous of versions of definition cannot be resolved and singular version to the topic would be disingenuous. So in lack of consensus of opinions it would be proper to put forth a cursory look on some of the vital arguments.

International encyclopedia of information and library science (Routledge, 2003) defines information science as a discipline that investigates the characteristics of information and the nature of the information transfer process, whilst not losing sight of the practical aspects of collecting, collating and evaluating information and organizing the dissemination through appropriate intellectual apparatus and technology.

According to Taylor, Information Science is a science that investigates the properties and behavior of information. It deals with the forces that govern the flow of information and the means of processing information for optimal accessibility and usability.

Summers put forth the view that information science comprises a library without walls; its "collection" is the entire world of information and the "information scientist" acquires, organizes, and disseminates that information to help people meet their needs.

Brittain argues that information science is characterized as "deinstitutionalized library science".

Borko opines that information science is a field of professional practice and scientific inquiry addressing the problem of effective communication of knowledge records among humans in the context of social, organizational, and individual need for and use in information.

Contrary to the above arguments, White and McClain argue that information science is a interface between people and literature. Information science models the world of publication with a practical goal of being able to deliver their content on demand to inquirers.

H. Bose concludes that information science is recognized as a complex multidisciplinary subject ranging computers and telecommunication through cybernetics to psychology, logic and techniques of classification and indexing, and as professional discipline concerned with the accumulation, storage and transfer of recorded knowledge.

According to Slamecka information science is an interdisciplinary field of study of the nature, properties, control and use of information.

On the other hand, Wersig uses the term 'post modern science' in lieu of information science as he finds it to be driven by the need to develop strategies to solve the problems caused by the classical science and technologies.

Wilson opines that information science is that set of practices and related disciplinary studies which is concerned with the generation, transmission, organization, storage, retrieval and use of information together with the studies of the user of information.

According to Fairthorne The whole group of applied disciplines together with their pertinent fundamental disciplines forming the foundation of information generation, communication and service systems may well be viewed as federation of disciplines or information science.

According to Mccrank, 2002 history as science is an information science. Its speciality is informimg the present about the past.

However, Mansfield critics the arguments and argues that the term 'information' and 'science' are both ambiguous. According to him information science is being used to describe heterogeneous set of activities, so called information science forcing the search for a unifying conceptual framework where none exists.

Tefko Saracevic in Interdisciplinary nature of information science Ciência da Informação - Vol 24, número 1, 1995 – Artigos has put forth three pivotal characteristics that serve as a framework for understanding the past, present and future of information science.

According to him these three general characteristics are the leitmotifs of its very evolution and existence. These are shared with many modern fields.

First, information science is interdisciplinary in nature; however, the relations with various disciplines are changing. The interdisciplinary evolution is far from over.

Second, information science is inexorably connected to information technology. A technological imperative is compelling and constraining the evolution of information science, as is the evolution of information society.

Third, information science is, with many other fields, an active participant in the evolution of information society. Information science has a strong social and human dimension, above and beyond the technology.

GENESIS OF INFORMATION SCIENCE

The term 'information science' came into practice in the 1950s. The aftermath of Second World War led to wealth of information. There was a need to handle and counter the exponential and unabated information growth. According to Encyclopedia of information and library science (Routledge, 2003) to meet the approaching challenges some scientist started specializing in information. It stemmed into a new class of information workers called literature chemist. In 1940 the generic term information scientist was used to describe the new class of people having mastered the art of handling information. Chris Hanson of Aslib in 1956 referred the work of these people as information science as there was a vast difference in their nature from the traditional custodians of information viz. librarians. By 1960s sufficient number of people felt the need of information science and founded institute of information scientist to provide specialist education as well as formulation of standards.

According to Shera the name information science derived in the first place from Shannon's information theory and its popularization by Weaver (which received wide publicity at the end of 1940s).

FORMS OF INFORMATION SCIENCE

Information Science and technology abstracts identified eleven major categories of information science. These are:

- Information science research
- Knowledge organization
- Information profession
- Societal issues
- Information industry
- Publishing and distribution
- Information technology
- Electronic information system and services
- Subject specific courses and application
- Libraries and library services
- Government and legal information issues.

FEATURES OF INFORMATION SCIENCE

1. It focuses on the information phenomenon regardless of the format or context.
2. It stresses on the information transfer cycle from creation to use.
3. Its root traces out from interdisciplinary fields.

CONTRIBUTIONS OF INFORMATION SCIENCE

1. It developed a specific field called bibliometrics for measuring the information explosion. Bibliometrics encompasses many aspects like impact factor, bibliographic coupling, citation and co-citation patterns.
2. It restrained the exponential and unabated information growth curve. The dilapidated information sector was blessed with the developments like automatic indexing

and abstracting, KWIC and KWOC indexing, citation indexing, natural language searching and controlled vocabularies.

3. It developed online database system to avoid data redundancy accompanied by the developments in networking and searching techniques.
4. Development and formulation of standards for information processing and communication as well as administering national information infrastructure.

CHARACTERISTICS OF INFORMATION SCIENCE

1. Interdisciplinary nature where the relations with other disciplines are continuously changing and evolving.
2. It is highly affluence by information technology
3. Its active involvement leads to information society.

APPLICATIONS OF INFORMATION SCIENCE

According to ALA encyclopedia of reference services (ALA,1996) there are two applications of information science: logistical and process oriented.

1. Logistical application-Accounting of commodities
   (a) Database creation
   (b) Online information services
2. Process orientation-Human use of commodities
   (a) Management information systems
   (b) Command-control-communication systems
   (c) Decision support system
   (d) Expert system

LIBRARY SCIENCE & INFORMATION SCIENCE

It is modish to demarcate borders between library science and information science. In the earlier sections we saw data, information and knowledge as a continuous spectrum. Similarly, librarians and information scientist are dedicated to generation, use and transfer of knowledge. Like their traditional counterparts, who are engaged in information activities, information science are engaged in knowledge business. Further, a library scientist are properly educated and well trained to serve the people while, an information scientist is interested in increasing the capability of library through available technology. Information system is a signal term used to represent the objectives of an information scientist.

Summers have also put forth three core concerns of library science that found its solution from the information science. They are:

I. *Storage*: Digital libraries

II. *Communication*: Information retrieval and intelligent agent interaction.

III. *Use*: Knowledge management

INTERDISCIPLINARY PERSPECTIVE TO INFORMATION SCIENCE

The interdisciplinary framework of information science has provided depth and breadth to its scope and nature of study. Interdisciplinary approach in information science was introduced and is being kept alive to the present by the richness of articulated differences in addressing the problems. Differences in background were and are difficult to figure out. Moreover, it has contributed to both richness of the field as well as difficulties in its communication and education. People working in the background of every discipline made an equally relevant contribution, but its mishmash was responsible for sustaining a strong interdisciplinary characteristic of information science. Further, information science was swamped by plenitude of subjects.

It is important as modern society increasingly demands application-oriented knowledge, and the usability of scientific knowledge generally requires the combination and integration of knowledge form various scientific disciplines.

"According to Stember Information Science has incorporated a number of distinct disciplines into its mainstream and peripheral research. Given that information science has multiple disciplines at work within it, there is an immediate need to investigate the nature and value of collaboration of various subjects. A major component of this investigation is clarifying semantic meaning for terms that are frequently used interchangeably by researchers and practitioners with no clarification: intradisciplinary, crossdisciplinary, multidisciplinary, transdisciplinary and interdisciplinary"

The subjects that exhibit interdisciplinary relations with information science are: education, computer science, communication, cognitive science, mathematics, language and artificial intelligence.

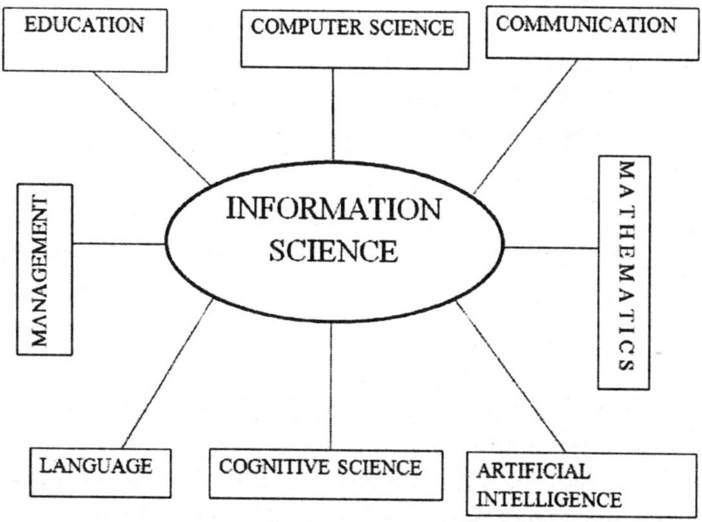

COMPUTERS

As information science is related with the storage and

retrival of information, computer are known for mass storage and searching along with processing. Computer enables the access of information from multiple destinations simultaneously.

All routine jobs like acquisition, cataloguing, serial control, circulation etc to information services like CAS, SDI, retrospective search, online databases are related with computers

PSYCHOLOGY

Psychology is the study of mind- the way we think, act, feel, and develop. Psychology as a science attempts to describe, predict and explain thought and behavior using the scientific methods. Psychology is a fused product of philosophy and physiology. It is probably the most interdisciplinary field among modern interdisciplinary field. The fields that compose psychology, while bringing different approaches, share a basic concern about understanding cognitive processes, their realization in the brain, the structure of the mind, and various manifestation of the mind, such as intelligence. The significance of cognitive science lies in interaction of different approaches to these most complex and intriguing problems.

Psychology plays an important role in information service. Information service should be based on uers needs and assessment. Knowledge of psychology helps to understand the user correctly, treat in appropriately, analyse his problem or need precisely and provide the scientific information most suitable to the users.

Yet another area where knowledge of human psychology has a definite role to play is designing or developing an information retrieval system. The indexer has to select a term which majority of the users are likely to use and he should also provide cross references from all the alternative terms under which users are likely to search.

Some of the concern areas of psychology influenced by information science are:

1. Logic
2. Information need
3. Cognitive science
4. Techno stress/ergonomics
5. Library use studies [likert scale]
6. Semiotics

MATHEMATICS

Mathematics is the science dealing with quantity, for measurement and arrangements and in particular with the methods for discovering by concepts and models. Various information models are developed particularly in information technology with use of the mathematical expressions.

There are various branches of information science where mathematics and its principles are heavily used- such as bibliometrics, scientometrics, webometrics and informetrics.

It is also used in measurement and evaluation of information systems and services. Various ratios such as recall, precision etc are expressed by the use of ratio analysis drawn from mathematics

LINGUISTICS

Linguistics is the study of language. Linguistics is of great significance in information processing. In the process of indexing the indexer has to choose the terms from the natural language. Such terms should match the vocabulary of the text and search terms of the users.

Language makes representation of information easy and converts information to an explainable entity. The other areas where linguistics play an important role are: compilation of bibliographies, translation (both manual and mechanical), transliteration, abstracting etc. Thus linguistics play an important role in documentation and information work.

Language has an edge over the needs of information scientists as:

a. It is an important tool in representing, classifying and categorizing events.

b. It is a means of communication that is a basis of all information and knowledge.

Some of the developments in the language with the influence of information science are:

1. GIST cards
2. UTF (Universal true font)
3. Unicode
4. Internet linguistics

MANAGEMENT

The term 'management' encompasses an array of different functions undertaken to accomplish a task successfully. It is the way and the process of how one achieves ones target or goals and it is in this respect that management is considered an art and a science as well. Management is all about:

Managing-men-tactfully

Managing-men-technology

Managing-men-as team

Managing-competencies

Managing-objectives

Managing-objectives

Information science has affluence the aspects of management at its best and developed new tools for enhancing the managerial practices:

1. Management information system

2. Decision support system
3. Expert system

METHODS OF INFORMATION SCIENCE

By the methods of information science it means how the information professional moves ahead in his areas of interest especially in research and for decision making. This concept was introduced by Chris Hanson of Aslib in 1956.

CLASSICAL METHODS

There are two classical methods:

1. Deductive method : Observable facts are removed considering it as true without requiring the proof. From the great thinkers like Plato and Aristotle comes a tradition of dealing with uncertainty. Emphasis is placed on logic or deductive thinking.

2. Inductive thinking : The inductive method, however starts with observation from which a hypothesis (or guess) is generated. The hypothesis is tested through experimentation to affirm or negate it.

The procedure that is used to conduct the investigation or observation or study is referred to as scientific method. An important aspect of scientific method is the generation of a hypothesis about the phenomena in question.

Then, comes out the data collection through surveys, questionnaire, interviews and polls.

These four methods are grouped together because often survey is done using questionnaire, interview and polls.

Sampling : Sampling simply means determining the characteristics of the population that one wishes to study or investigate. It includes the number of individuals to be studied in addition to their characteristics so as to render results reliable and valid.

Critical discourse : Information professionals use opinions and comment among themselves as part of their approaches for understanding events and experiences.

Brainstorming : Brainstorming is a process in which new ideas and concepts emerge through mutual exchange. Implied in the process is that the outcome of the experience will provide insight to the problems or issues at hand.

Case history : A case history is a detailed account of the processes and outcomes associated with a particular phenomenon.

Models, Simulations and exercises : These are other ways through which information professionals make decisions in computer situation. Building a model or developing a simulation is often much less expensive and risky than building an information system based on untested hypothesis. Gaming is another effective tool for this.

Statistical methods : Once data is collected, the information professionals must determine their significance. Numerous statistical methods can be applied to data evaluation like measure of central tendency, variability, linear models and regression analysis. Various software packages are also available like MS-Excel, SPSS etc.

REFERENCES

1. Bose,H. Information Science: principles and practice New York:Envoy press, 1986
2. Slamecka,V. Information Science Generally and Specifically Southeastern librarian.15,1965,pp.15-18
3. Wersig,G. Information science: the study of postmodern knowledge usage Information processing and management 29,1993, pp.229-239
4. Wilson,T.D. Sociological aspects of information science INT Forum Information Documentation 6,1981,pp13-18
5. Fairthorne,R.A. The scope and aims of information sciences and technologies (In Mikhailov, A.I and others;Ed. On theoretical problems of informatrics.) pp.25-31.

6. Saracevic, Tefko Interdisciplinary nature of information science Ciência da Informação - Vol 24, número 1, 1995 – Artigos
7. Shera, J.H.(1968). Of librarianship, documentation and information science. Unesco Bulletin for libraries, 22(2),1968,pp.55-65
8. Bottle, R.T. and Efthimiandes, E.N. Library and information science literature: authorship and growth patterns, Journal of Information science 9; 107-16
9. Montanelli, D.S. and Mak, C. Library practitioners use of literature, Library tends, 1988, 36: 765-83
10. Wellisch, H. (1972) From information science to informatics: a terminological investigation, Journal of librarianship 4: 157-87
11. Wersig, G. (1993) Information science: the study of post modern knowledge usage, Information processing and management 29: 229-39
12. Vickery, B. (1999) A century of scientific and technical information, Journal of Documentation 55: 476-527
13. Warner, J. (2001) W(h)ither information science?/! The Library Quarterly 71:231-42
14. Allen, Bryce L. (1991) Cognitive research in information science: implications for design. ARIST 26:3-37
15. Brittain, J.M. The distinctive characteristics of Information science. In Theory and applications of information research: proceedings of the second international research forum on information science. Edited by Ole Harbo and Leif Kajberg. London:Mansell, 1980.
16. Rayward, Boyd Library and Information Sciences In The Study of Information Interdisciplinary Messages. EDiteed by Fritz Machlup and Una Mansfield. New York: Wiley, 1983, 343-363.
17. Shera, Jesse H. and Donald B. Cleveland History and foundations of information science and technology. Vol. 12. Edited by Martha E. Williams.Knowledge Industry, 1977, 249p.
18. Wellisch, Hans. From Information Science to Informatics: a terminological investigation. Journal of librarianship 4 (July 1972): 157-187
19. Brookes,B.C. The foundation of information science J.ISc 1980,2(3-4),125-133
20. G.Bhattacharya in Information Sciences : a unified view through a system approach (IASLIC, 1978)
21. Nauta,Doedi The meaning of information Mounton:The Hague,1972

22. Losee,Robert A discipline independent definition of information science J.ISc 1997,48(3), 254-269

23. Pratt,Allan The information of the image: a model of the communication process Libri 1977,27(3),204-220,

24. Derr,Richard The concept of information in ordinary discourse Information process management 1985,21(6),489-499

25. Mansfield, Una The wider scope of information research, (Current trends in information: research and theory, Bill Katz and Robin Kinder eds.) New York: Haworth, 1987,p.64

26. Debons, A. Foundations of Information Science. In Information: An integrated view. Boston, Mass:G.K. Hall,1980

27. International Encyclopaedia of Information and Library Science. (2003). London: Routledge

28. Encyclopaedia of Library and Information Science (2010) New York: CRC Press.

5
Information Productivity Metrics

The preceding chapters embodied the theoretical implications of the information. Information is an intangible product of human intellect which can neither be seen nor felt but can be only expressed. Numerous attempts were undertaken for the qualitative expression and quantification of information behavior. It led to a separate field of study called Information Metrics where prime importance was to imply statistics to the scholarly works. Although information is immeasurable yet, it achieved biggest breakthrough in information quantification by devising tools to measure the productivity of authors, journals, scientific collaborations and the citation counts. Information metrics includes the art of metrical composition of productivity of scientific works. In other words it deals with application of statistics and mathematical analysis to productivity.

Voyage of Information Productivity Metrics

Over a period of time, several terms were coined devoted to more or less the same thing: statistical bibliography to librametry to bibliometrics/ scientometrics to informetrics. New terms were partly coined because the parent subject underwent drastic changes during the last 2-3 decades. The change was from library science to documentation and then to information science or information studies. The changes were due to the impact of Information Technology and the inter-disciplinary nature of the subject. The quantitative studies in information productivity witnessed varied nomenclature with varying time periods. It started with statistical analysis by Cole & Eale in 1917. In 1923, E.W. Hulme used the term statistical bibliography but it was a vague term. However, the seed of metrics in the information world was put forth by S.R. Ranganathan at the Aslib conference at Lemington Spa in 1948 where he put forth the term "Librametry or Librametrics" on the line of psychometrics or econometrics as library works involved large numbers.

Derek J. de Solla Price pioneering work Little Science, Big Science (1963) hugely impacted the study of scientific growth productivity and laid the foundations of bibliometrics studies. He used "little science" to refer to modest group of learned scholars and "big science" for the huge investment in scientific infrastructure and skills. Further he concluded that with the scientific growth there is profuse growth in the scientific productivity and the number of scientists.

The term bibliometrics was first used by Alan Pritchard in 1969 in his article "Statistical Bibliography or Bibliometrics" in 1969 which is accepted till date by the information professionals and the learned scholars although Paul Otlet had previously employed the term "bibliometrie" in 1934. Nonetheless, the first manifestation of bibliometrics is found in 1873 when de Candolle predicted the dynamicity of scientific strength of nations according to membership of scientific societies. With this study he aimed to identify factors that might influence the scientific success of a nation (van Raan, 2004). Afterwards, Lotka (1926) analysed the "frequency distribution of scientific productivity" that led to the development of Lotka`s law. Another trailblazer endeavor in this field was Gross and Gross (1927) study of "citation analysis" whose aim was to identify those journals which have high impact in their research field chemistry. This study brought mountainous ripples to metric studies and citation analysis became an inescapable phenomenon. It was further supplemented by Bradford (1934) who contemplated "journal productivity" and preferred frequency distribution of papers across journals. Another pioneering work was of Zipf (1935, 1949) which is a generalized approach to Lotka`s and Bradford`s law who studied the "frequency of words in a text". Anyhow the quantum leap of metric studies was brought by the Garfield`s (1955) "Science Citation Index" database.

Bibliometrics

It is a branch of metric studies which attempts to explore the quantitative behavior of information. Etymologically bibliometrics comprises two terms: (Biblion and metrics). Biblion is a latin word that means book or paper whereas, metrics is a greek word that means science of meter or measurement. According to Alan Pritchard application of mathematical methods to books and other media of communication is bibliometrics. In other words, all studies which seek to quantify written communication is bibliometrics. Traditionally it was associated with the quantitative measurement of documented materials only. People considered it as a citation or publication driven tool to gauge scientific productivity or compilation of cleaned-up bibliographies on research domains extended by citation data. However, the earlier notions of (Thelwall,2009) bibliometrics has changed out of all recognition since 1958, becoming established as a field, being taught widely in library and information science schools, and being at the core of a number of science evaluation research groups around the world.

First landmark to quantitative assessment of scholarly literature was brought by the creation of ISI citation database in 1962. Since then there has been a continuous increase in the computing power available in universities which has helped to make increasing numbers of bibliometric analyses possible. The second breakthrough was brought was the web publishing of broad range of research related documents allowing the creation of a range of new metrics relating to their access and use. (Thelwall, 2009).

Bibliometric study can be grouped into three broad categories:

1. Descriptive bibliometrics : It studies the number of publications in a field or the literature productivity of that field to portray a comparative account of literature production during varied time range or the share of literature produced in sub domains of the field. This study is primarily based on numerical count of papers, books and other documented scholarly works which have been abstracted in specialized abstracting journals.

Study in descriptive bibliometrics primarily deals with the productivity count relating to geographic variations, time period and disciplines.

2. Evaluative bibliometrics : It deals with the study of usage of literature by researcher worker in a given field.It is carried by counting the references cited by research workers in their scholarly thought contents. Study in evaluative bibliometrics fundamentally deals with literature usage count that is based on reference and citation count.

3. Relational bibliometrics : These are used in scientific research for examining relations through the use of ISI data. Lack of computing power and technical-knowhow had paralyzed such study earlier. This idea, says Telwall (2008), came from geneticist Allen in 1960, who sent his citation diagram to Garfield (Cawkell, 2000). Journal citation diagrams could illustrate the connections between journals within a field, both central and peripheral. This idea led to the development of co-citation as a tool to measure similarity by Garfield. It connotes that if in any scholarly work two documents are found to appear together in the reference lists (co-cited), then there thought content are likely to be somewhat similar.

Bibliometric studies can help us to achieve the following:

a) Determine the core journals in a field/ Scattering of a journal

b) Ranking of Journals (Determination of Impact factor)

c) Selection and Weeding of Journals

d) Identification of growth of literature

e) Trends in a subject

f) Determination of author's productivity, organizational productivity, and countries productivity

g) Geographic distribution of literature

h) Time consumed in generation of literature

According to Mattison (2008) bibliometrics is used as a methodology in many other scientific fields to map the publication pattern in various disciplines. Philosophically, bibliometrics contributes to a better understanding of the information universe because it is the study of how humans relate to information (Bates, 1999)

In nutshell, it can be surmised that by employing various kinds of statistical methods to the books and documents one can better understand and use literature in various fields of study. Bibliometric studies have emerged as an inevitable tool for studying the research collaborations. Modern research is an inter-disciplinary endeavor where knowledge, technical skills and innovative ideas among researchers of variant disciplines are complemented by each other.Collaborative research works besides enabling the sharing and pooling up of resources for enhanced efficiency also contribute to the quality of research outcome (Matteson et. al, 2008). Funding agencies of national and international importance have also understood its significance and are developing interdisciplinary research centres for collaborative research.

Bibliometric tools

Tool	Purpose	Type
Bibliometrics toolbox	A set of computer programs, written in Turbo Pascal developed by Terrence A. Brookes that measures the bibliometric aspects of a literature such as Bradfordity, productivity ranks, degree of clustering, and indices of concentration	Computer program
Dataview	It is a bibliometric software for analyzing downloaded data from the databases.	Software
Bibexcel	A toolbox developed by Olle Persson to generate data files that can be imported to excel or any program that takes tabbed data records for further processing.	Software
BibTechMon	Commercial software designed to assist in analyzing bibliographic data.	Software
Sitkis	It utilizes bibliometric data exported from ISI web of Science for descriptive statistics.	Software
Metric	It is used to harvest bibliometric data in European national bibliographical databases.	Software

Laws of Bibliometrics

The major empirical laws of bibliometrics are Lotka's law, Bradford Law and Zipf's law. They are the ones that have been used most often in the literature to model the distribution of information phenomena (Chen & Leimkuhler, 2006). These laws serve as an indispensable tool for library and information science to predict the patterns and analyze the recorded information and communications. On the basis of such studies Jayroe (2008) opines that libraries can then develop theories on why certain structures and patterns occur, subsequently creating practices that enable the best use of information behaviour based on those findings.

Lotka's Law of Scientific productivity or Inverse Square Law of Scientific Productivity

The statistical analysis of scientific literature began almost 50 years before the term "Bibliometrics" was coined. Alfred J. Lotka chemist, demographer, ecologist and mathematician in 1926 published his pioneering study on the frequency distribution of scientific productivity of authors determined from decennial index of Chemical Abstracts from 1907-1916 and the name index of Auerbach`s Geschichtestaflen der Physik to find out the publication productivity of authors in the domains of Physics and Chemistry. He concluded that "the number of authors making n contributions is about $1/n^2$ of those making one; and the proportion of all contributors that make a single contribution is about 60 percent"

This means that out of all the authors in a given field, 60% will have just one publication, and 15% will have two publications as:

$$N=1/2^2$$
$$=1/4 = 15$$

and 7% authors will have three publications and so on.

For example,

Let us consider the case of Journal of Finance.

Total number of authors who wrote during 1948-1988= 1844 authors

STEP: I

Calculate total contribution during the period.

Out of 1844 authors,

1237 = Contributed 1 article during 1948-1988

295 = Contributed 2 article during 1948-1988

140 = Contributed 3 article during 1948-1988

63 = Contributed 4 article during 1948-1988

41 = Contributed 5 article during 1948-1988

68 = Contributed 6 or more article during 1948-1988

STEP: II

Calculate the percentage of contributions.

Percentage of author contributing 1 article during 1948-1988

= 1237/1844 × 100

= 67.1%

Percentage of author contributing 2 articles during 1948-1988

= 295/1844 × 100

= 16%

Percentage of author contributing 3 articles during 1948-1988

= 140/1844 × 100

= 7.6%

Percentage of author contributing 4 articles during 1948-1988

= 63/1844 × 100

= 3.4%

Percentage of author contributing 5 articles during 1948-1988

= 41/1844 × 100

= 2.2%

Percentage of author contributing 6 articles during 1948-1988

= 68/1844 × 100

= 3.7%

Lotka's formulae to determine author productivity:

$X^n.y$ = constant

Where, x = number of publications

Y = number of authors contributing × publications

STEP: III

Calculation using the formulae

Using the formulae, $X^n.y = C$

$$(1)^2.67 = 67$$

$$(2)^2.16 = 64$$

$$(3)^2.7 = 63$$

$$(4)^2.3 = 48$$

$$(5)^2.2 = 50$$

Henceforth, we find that the value of C ranges from 48 to 67. Since the limit was fixed Lotka called it to be constant.

A graph can be plotted between the numbers of authors to that of publications.

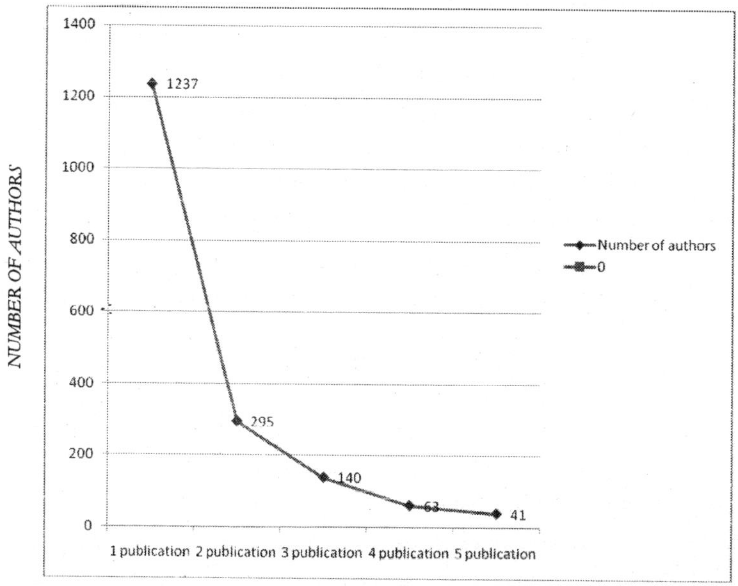

Lotka's law when applied to large bodies of literature over a long period of time can be accurate in general but not statistically exact. But, even after more than 87 years after its publication the law is considered as the rule of thumb. The only condition that needs to be assumed in Lotka's law is the time period. If we expect to find a small group of prolific authors it is necessary to consider a long enough time period so that they have enough opportunity to publish more than once or twice which is set at 10 or more years (Andres, 2009). Lotka's law can be applied in generating the statistics of productivity of authors, organizations and countries over different fields of subject area.

Bradford's Law of Scattering

Eight years after Lotka's article appeared, Bradford (1934) published his study on the frequency distribution of paper over journal.

Before understanding this law, we will have to understand the process of scattering, which is the phenomenon in which the literature on specific subject is published in the journal of other related subjects. Bradford law serves as a general guideline to librarians in determining the number of core journals in any given field. Bradford's law states that journals in a single field can be divided into three parts, each containing the same number of articles:

1. A core of journals on the subject relatively few in number, that produces one-third of all the articles.
2. A second zone, containing the same number of articles, but greater number of journals.
3. A third zone, containing the same number of the second, but a still greater number of journals.

Bradford Scattering Zones : In any field of study the journals can be grouped into three zones:

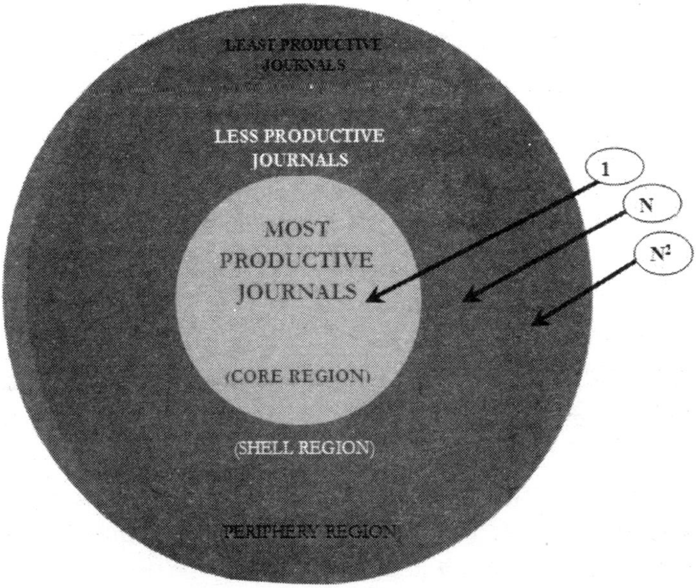

Core region: It consists of the most productive share of journals on subject. In this region the number of journals as well as the relevant articles is same as shell and periphery region.

Shell region: It consist of less productive journals on a subject. Here, the number of articles is same however the number of relevant journals to that of core region is doubled.

Periphery region: It consists of the least productive journals on a subject. It contains equal number of articles but the number of relevant journal is much more compared to the core and periphery region.

Bradford expressed this relation as:

$1: n: n^2$

Core region: Shell region: Periphery region

Most Productive Journals: Less Productive Journals: Least Productive Journals

Bradford formulated his law after studying a bibliography of Geo-physics, covering 326 journals in the field.

He discovered that:

9 journals contained 429 articles

59 journals contai8ned 499 articles

258 journals contained 404 articles

So, it took 9 journals to produce almost one third of the articles, 5 times 9 or 45 to produce the next third and 5 times 5 times 9, or 225 to produce the last third. So, Bradford law is also not statistically accurate.

Bradford law is commonly known as 20:80law which means that 20% of the core journals are producing 80% of the articles of that particular subject area and 80% of the articles of the related areas produce 20% of the articles due to scattering

It enables the librarians to determine the core journals of a particular subject field. Thus, helps in subscription/ unsubscription and weeding of journals in the library.

Zipf's Law of word frequency distribution

Zipf's law (1949) is often used to predict the frequency of words within a text. This law states that "list the words occurring within that text in order decreasing frequency, the rank of a word on that list multiplied by its frequency will equal a constant.

The equation for this relationship is:

$$r \times f = k$$

Where, r = rank of the words

f = Frequency

k = Constant.

Usage of Zipf's law (Loose, 1990)

1. Gather up the keyterms or words of your interest.
2. For each word find out an estimation of the frequency of occurrence of each key terms or words.

3. Rank the key terms or words in the descending order with the most frequently occurring type ranked one.
4. Organize the term distribution data:

Terms	Rank (r)	Frequency (f)	(r) × (f)	(r) × (f) = constant calculated	Predicted
The	1	810	1 x 810	810	1000
Of	2	450	2 x 450	900	550
A	3	280	3 x 280	840	330
information	4	270	4 x 270	1080	250
is	5	230	5 x 230	1150	200
to	6	200	6 x 200	1200	170
and	7	190	7 x 190	1330	143
that	8	170	8 x 170	1360	128
as	9	160	9 x 160	1440	110
in	10	140	10 x 140	1400	100
we	11	130	11 x 130	1430	91
be	12	125	12 x 125	1500	85
or	13	90	13 x 90	1170	77
may	14	85	14 x 85	1190	71
by	15	80	15 x 80	1200	65
can	16	75	16 x 75	1200	60
society	17	70	17 x 70	1190	58
education	18	65	18 x 65	1170	56
training	19	60	19 x 60	1140	52
profession	20	55	20 x 55	1100	50

5. Apply the formula, r × f = constant

Where, r = rank of word

f – frequency (number of times the given word is used in the context)

c = constant for the given text

6. Estimate the constant c. Here I have estimated c= 1000. Note how thw values are close to 1100.
7. Plot the distributions (Calculated and Predicted) with the rank on the X-axis and the frequency on the Y-axis.

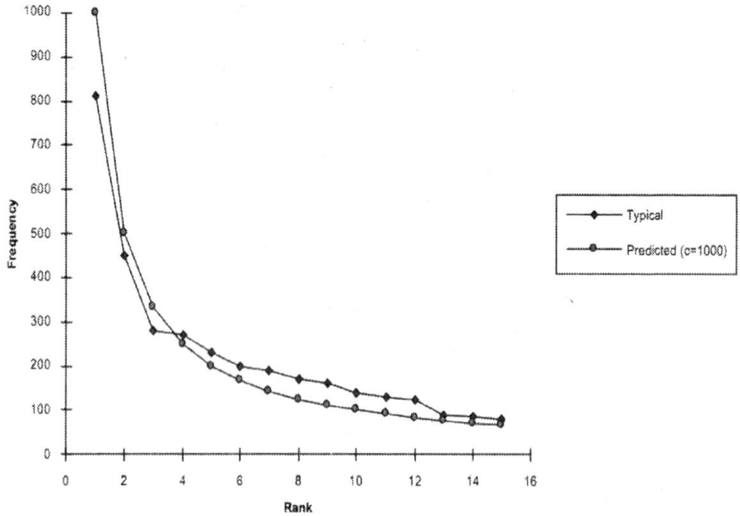

Proximity of Laws of Bibliometrics

Bibliometric studies has been subjected to be a contested project for the learned scholars. Most of the savants argue that the three pioneering works of Lotka, Bradford and Zipf are more the less same in nature. Chen and Leimkuhler (1986) showed the mathematical equivalence of Lotka's, Bradford's and Zipf's law. All three laws relate via a simple function and two variables:

Laws	Observations		Subject of Study
Lotka's law	Number of authors	Number of papers	Author
Bradford's law	Number of journals	Number of related papers	Journal
Zipf's law	Number of words in a text	Frequency of occurrence	Word

(Hubert, 1981) asserts that all the three laws study the

particular arrangement of two groups. Some scholars argue that the bibliometrics laws share similar mathematical grounds to study the information productivity. Table given below illustrates the scholars who agree with the same.

Scholars	Lotka's law	Bradford's law	Zipf's law
Kendall (1960)		✓	✓
Brookes (1968, 1969)		✓	✓
Fairthorne (1969)		✓	✓
Wikinson (1973)		✓	✓
Egghe (1991, 2005)	✓	✓	✓
Bookstein (1976)	✓		✓

Scientometrics

The term scientometrics came to prominence as the name of a journal founded by T. Braun in 1977 originally published in Hungary and now in Amsterdam (Tague-Sutcliffe, 1992). However, the term scientometrics was coined in 1969 by Nalimov and Mulcenko in Russian as "naukometrija". It assays the quantitative aspects of the scientific information`s use, dissemination and production to portray scientific researches as a social activity. It is analogous to bibliometric studies.

Scientometrics includes all quantitative aspects of the science of science, communication in science, and science policy (Wilson, 2001).

According to Pouris (1989), 'Scientrometrics is a application of quantitative techniques(system analysis, mathematical and statistical techniques etc.) to scientific communication(science output, science policy, science administration etc.) with the objectives of;

I. Developing science indicators;

II. Measuring the impact of science on society; and

III. Comparing the output as well as the impact of science at national and international levels.

Scientometric studies are dedicated to the scholarly papers and patents in public domain which are the immediate and intangible Science & Technology output. It deals with evaluative and analytical account of scientific and technological information as well as graphical representation of "Who is doing, what and where?"

Scientometric tools

The quantitative as well as qualitative analysis of any Scientometrics study, such as citation mapping, visualization, bibliographic coupling, co- authorship network, co-words mapping etc. are carried out by using Scientometrics tools. This tools are very much useful for Scientrometricians for mapping their parameters in any accept of their study. The quantitative as well as qualitative analysis of any Scientometrics study, such as citation mapping, visualization, bibliographic coupling, co-authorship network, co-words mapping etc. are carried out by using Scientometrics tools. This tools are very much useful for Scientrometricians for mapping their parameters in any accept of their study

Tool	Purpose	Type
Authormap	It is used for citation mapping and visualization	Web tool
Bibcouple	It is used for visualization of the bibliographic coupling among authors	Software Application
BibJourn	It is used to indicate the knowledge base of a document set.	Software Application
Citespace	It is used for visualizing patterns and trends in scientific literature	Map
CleanPop	It is used to clean systematically the result from Publish or Perish tool	Web tool
Co-auth	It is used to generate a representation of co-authorship relations in a document set	Software application

Fulltext	It is software for co-word mapping of full texts	Software application
IlitCite	Bibliographic analysis and visualization software	Software
IntColl	It is used to generate a representation of international co-authorship relations in a document set	Software application
ISI	It is freely available for academic usage. It is used for organizing a set downloaded from the Web-of-Science into databases for relational database management.	Software application
Publish or perish	It is a software program that retrieves and analyzes academic citations. It uses Google Scholar to obtain the raw citations	Software application
RefViz	It is a data visualization and analysis software from the makers of Endnote, ProCite, and Reference Manager for exploring reference collections	Software application
TI	It is used to generate a word-occurrence matrix and is available free for academic usage.	Software application

Some of the scientometrics measures and indices are as under

Index	Brain-child	Year	Definition/Mathematical Expression
h-index	Hirsch	2005	It is used to measure the impact and productivity of the published work of a scholar or scientist. If we order the papers of an author in decreasing order of the number of citations received, then the h-index of this author equals h, if r=h is the highest rank such that the first h papers each have h or more citations
g-index	Leo Egghe	2006	It is an index to quantify scientific

			productivity based on publication record. It states that "Given a set of articles ranked in a decreasing order of the number of citations that they received, the g-index is the unique largest number that the top g articles received together at least g^2 citations." Mathematically it can be expressed as: $g^2 \leq \sum_{i \leq g} c_i$
A index	Jin B.	2006	Mathematically it can be expressed as: $A = \frac{1}{h} \sum cit_j$
$h^{(2)}$ index	Kosmulkski	2006	
h_{norm} index	Sidiropoulos, Katsaros, and Manolopoulos	2007	Mathematically it can be expressed as: $h^n = \frac{h}{N_p}$
R index	Jin, B., Liang, L., Rousseau, R., & Egghe, L.	2007	Mathematically it can be expressed as: $R = \sqrt{\sum cit_j}$
AR index	Liang et al.	2007	Mathematically it can be expressed as: $AR = \sqrt{\sum \frac{cit_j}{a_j}}$
h_w index	Egghe and Rousseau	2007	Mathematically it can be expressed as: $h_w = \sqrt{\sum_{j=1}^{r_e} cit_j}$
e index	Zhang	2009	Mathematically it can be expressed as: $e = \sqrt{\sum cit_j - h^2}$

hg index	Alonso	2010	Mathematically it can be expressed as: $hg = \sqrt{h \times g}$
p index	Gagan Prathap	2010	Mathematically it can be expressed as: $p = h_m = \left(\frac{C^2}{P}\right)^{\frac{1}{3}}$

Cybermetrics

Quantitative studies pertaining to the nature of scientific communications over the Internet and its repercussions on the diffusion of ideas and information is known as cybermetrics.

The study of the quantitative aspects of the construction and use of information resources, structures and technologies on the whole Internet drawing on bibliometric and informetric approaches (Bjorneborn, 2004)

Bjorneborn and Ingwersen (2004) argues that Informatricians tend to agree that cybermetrics is a broader area that encompasses webometrics.

Cybermetric studies focuses on following scopes:

- Statistical aspects of the Web and the computer-interposed scholarly communication via web (Herring, 2002)
- Quantitative measurement and analysis of the Internet backbone technology, topology, and traffic (Molyneux and Williams, 1999)
- Analyis of Web contents, link structures and web usability
  - Cybergeography {Study of geography of computers that exists behind computer screens} and Cybercartography {New paradigm for mapping and mapmaking in the information era} (Dodge & Kitchin, 2001, 2002)
  - Web ecology {Scientific study of interactions

between one another and with the virtual world over the web} (Chi et al., 1998)

— Web mining {Mining of data from the web to discover patterns of the web} (Cooley, Mobasher, & Srivastava, 1997; Etzioni, 1996).

— Web graph analysis {Study of the link patterns emerging between documents and websites on the web} (Broader et al., 2000).

— Web dynamics {Study the changes. of web pages}(Levene & Poulovassilis, 2001)

— Web intelligence {Study of the application of Artificial intelligence and Information Technology on the web} (Yao, Zhong, Liu & Ohsuga, 2001)

Cybermetric Studies

Some of the cybermetric studies carried in the past are:

- Power law distributions
  - Study of web pages, inlinks, outlinks, visits per website (Adamic & Huberman, 2001)
- Corelation between research indicators and inlinks
  - Several studies by Thelwall et al. on U.K., Taiwan and Australia
  - EU projects: EICSTES + WISER
- Co-inlink cluster analysis
  - It is analogous to cocitation analysis.
  - Studies of Polanco et al. (2001) on EU universities and Vaughan & You on Chinese IT companies (2005)
- Longitudinal studies
  - Web page changes and permanence studies (Koehler, 2004)

Webometrics

The study of the quantitative aspects of the construction

and use of information resources, structures and technologies on the web drawing on bibliometric and informetric approaches (Bjorneborn, 2004). Several terms have used analogous to webometrics like: Netometrics (Bossy, 1995), Webometry (Abraham, 1996), Internetometrics (Almind & Ingwersen, 1996), Web bibliometry (Chakrabarti et al, 2002).

The coverage of webometric studies includes the following four main areas (Bjorneborn & Ingwersen, 2004):

- Web link structure analysis/ web colink analysis {Analysis of expanding hyperlinks collection of the unstructured information}
- Web page content analysis
- Web usage analysis
- Web technology analysis

According to Mitra and Cohen (1999) web can be considered as an object of study to understand the following facets:

- Inter-linkage
- Non-linearity
- Interactivity
- Multi-media
- Global reach
- Ephemerality

With the coming of the Web 2.0 "the participative web" i.e. an architecture of participation webometrics has given way to Webometrics 2.0 where blogometrics, wikimetrics, sociometrics and tagometrics studies are given prime importance.

Webometric tools

- User Focused (demand)
  - Focus groups
  - Surveys

- — User statistics tools: Hitwise, Sitemeter, Alexa, Google Analytics, Yahoo Analytics
- — Computer tracking devices: Phorm
- — Online SNA software: NodeXL

- Discourse analysis (It focuses on the web analysis as socio-cultural 'texts'.)

Informetrics

Informetrics is the study of quantitative aspects of information. This includes the production, dissemination and use of all forms of information, regardless of its forms or origin. The term "Informetrics" was coined by Otto Nacke in 1979. Informetrics is more about terminological differences that has arisen due to the lack of proper scholarly communication. Gorkova (1988) used the term informetrics to designate a more general sub-field of information science that dealt with the statistical analysis of communication process in science. Howeveer, Glanzel (2003) argues that Informetrics also deals with electronic media that includes the analysis carried out in electronic libraries.

The Library and Information Science field consist of informetrics, bibliometrics, scientometrics, cybermetrics and webometrics. These terminologies are frequently used interchangeably and leads to a chaotic state of terminologies. In a nutshell, informetrics field is a scientific discipline that includes all the statistical and mathematical aspects connected with library, documentation and information problems with strong links to the theoretical aspects of information retrieval.

Leo Egghe (2005) argues that "informetrics" is used as a broad term that comprises all metrics studies related to information science, including bibliometrics (bibliographies, librarie), scientometrics (science policy, citation analysis, research evaluation), webometrics (metrics f the web, the Internet or other social networks such as citation or collaboration networks.

Informetric studies deal with following areas:

- Scientometrics, which studies quantitative aspects of science.
- Webometrics, which studies quantitative aspects of the World Wide Web.
- Bibliometrics, which studies quantitative aspects of the recorded information.

Informetrics is an umbrella term for all the metrics study which embraces the overlapping filed of bibliometrics and scienctometrics. Webometrics is completely engulfed by bibliometric studies as web documents in their various forms such as text, multimedia are all recorded scholarly thought content stored on the web servers. Moreover, Webometrics is partially related to scientometrics because many scholarly activities in the science domain today are web-based. Cybermetrics completely eclipses webometrics but exceeds the boundaries of bibliometrics because some activities in the cyberspace are not normally recorded.

Thelwall, Vaughan and Bjorneboren in 2005 attempted to explained relationship between different metrics through the following diagram.

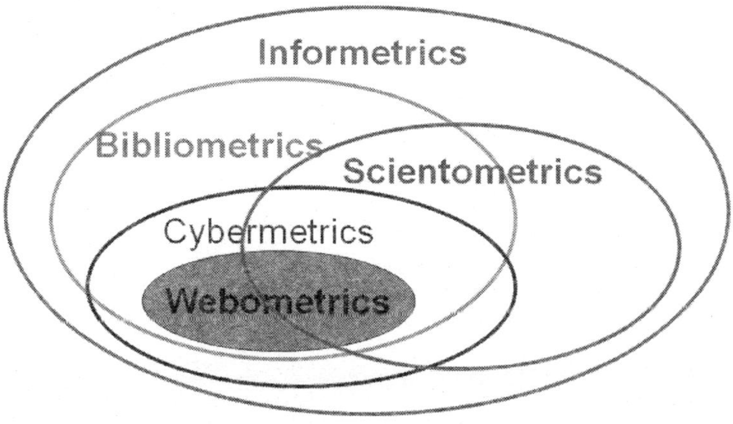

Leo Egghe and Ronald Rousseau have identified a place for Informetrics among other fields:

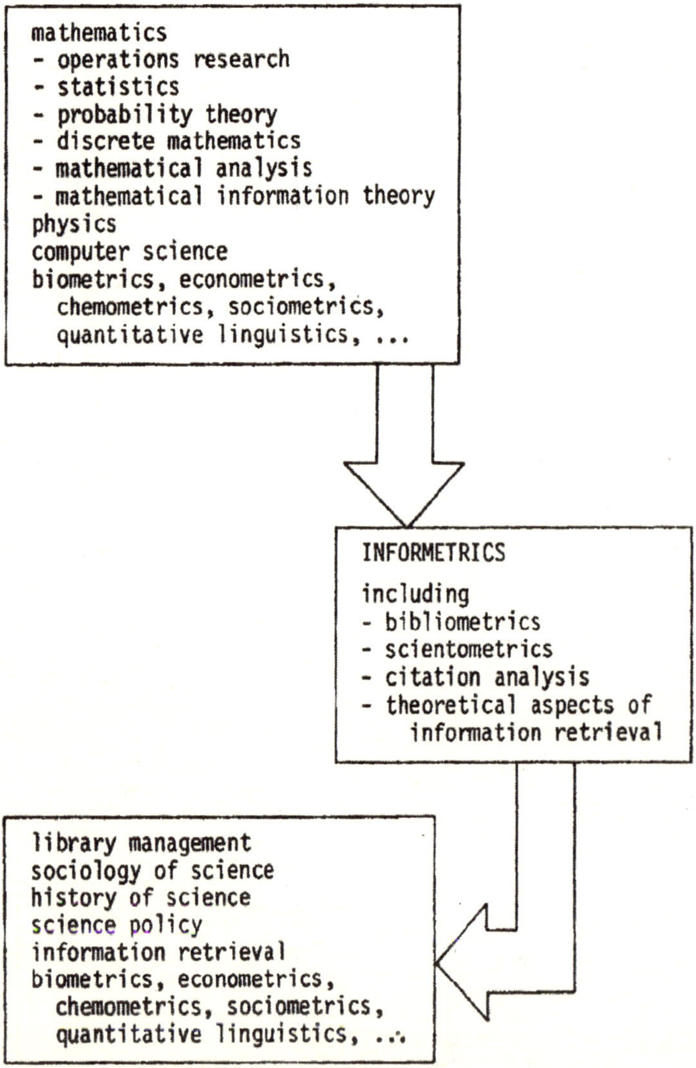

The subject and research areas of webometrics can be divided as:

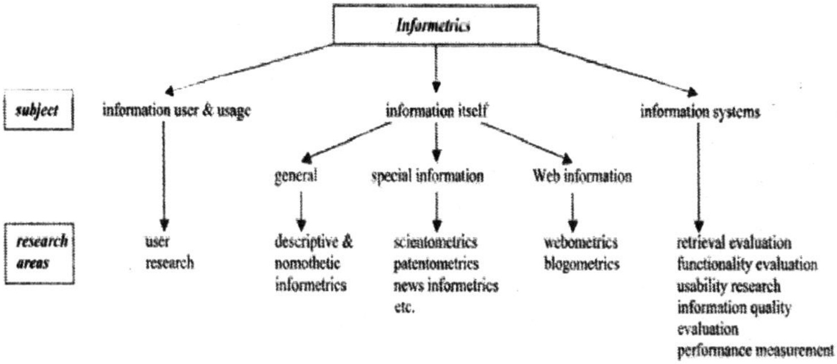

1. Information user and Usage

'User research' is a prime area of research in this subject area which mainly deals the topics on

- Human and their information behavior.
- Information seeking behavior on web (especially usage of search engine).
- Usage of library services.

2. Information System

Retrieval evaluation', 'Usability research' and 'Information quality' are major research areas in Information system.

- Retrieval evaluation is mainly involved in studying recall and precision of retrieval system.
- Usability research deals with tests of accessibility, accuracy, relevance, completeness, objectivity and timeliness of users.

3. Information Itself

Bibliometrics, Scientometrics and Webometrics are main research area in Information Itself.

REFERENCES

1. Ranganathan, S.R. Librametry and its scope. DRTC Seminar (7) paper DA. Bangalore:DRTC and Sarda Ranganathan Endowment of Library Science, 1969.

2. Price, D.J. (1963) Little Science, Big Science. New York: Columbia University Press.

3. De Candolle, A. (1873) Histoire des sciences et des savants depuis deux siecles. Geneva and Basle: H.Georg

4. Vaan Raan, A.F. J. (2004) Measuring science: Capita selecta of current main issues in H.F. Moed, W. Glanzel and U. Schmoch (eds), Handbook on Quantitative Science and Technology research. Dordrecht: Kluwer Academic

5. Gross, P.L.K. and Gross, E.M. (1927) College libraries and chemical education, Science, 66(1713), pp. 385-389.

6. Bradford, S.C. (1934) Sources of information on specific subjects, Engineering, 137, pp. 85-86.

7. Zipf, G.K. (1935) The Psycho-biology of Language. Cambridge, MA:MIT Press

8. Zipf, G.K. (1949) Human behaviour and the principle of least effort, Cambridge, MA: Addison-Wesley.

9. Garfield, E. (1955) Citation index for science- new dimension in documentation through association ideas, Science, 122(3159), pp. 108-111.

10. Thelwall, Mike(2009) Bibliometrics to webometrics In Information Science in transition Ed. By Alan Gilchrist ,UK:Facet

11. Bates, M. (1999) The invisible substrate of information science. Journal of the American Society of Information Science, 50(12) ,pp. 1043-1050

12. Mattison, P.(2009) Bibliometrics- an important tool in research evaluation. http://www.euroscience.org/bibliometrics-animportant-tool-in-research-evaluation,28

13. Mattison,P., Laget, P., Nilsson, A., and Sundberg, C.J. (2008) Intra-EU vs. extra-EU scientific collaborative patterns in EU. Scientometrics, 75(3), 555-574

14. Jayroe, Tina (2008) Bibliometrics for dummies

15. https://portfolio.du.edu/portfolio/getportfoliofile?uid=122400

16. Chen, Y. and Leimkuhler, F. (1986) A relationship between Lotka's law, Bradford's law, and Zipf's law. Journal of the American Society for Information Science, 37(5) 307-414.

17. Andres, Ana (2009) Measuring academic research: how to undertake a bibliometric study. Oxford:Chandos

18. Lotka A.J. (1926). The frequency distribution of scientific productivity. Journal of the Washington Academy of Sciences, 16: 317-323.

19. Losee, Robert M. 1990. The science of information. San Diego: Academic Press

20. Chen, Y.S. and Leimkuhler, F.F. (1986) a relationship between Lotka's, Bradford's and Zipf's law, JASIST, 37(5), pp. 307-314.

21. Hubert, J.J. (1981) General bibliometric models, Library Trends, 30(1), pp. 65-81.

22. Kendall, M.G. (1960) The bibliography of operational research, Operational research Quarterly, 11, pp. 31-36.

23. Tague-Sutcliffe, Jean (1992) An introduction to informetrics, Information Processing and Management, 28, pp. 1-3.

24. Wison, C.S. (2001) Informetrics In: M.E. Williams (Ed.) Annual Review of Information Science & Technology, Vol. 34, Mendford, NJ:Information Today., Inc. for the American Society of Information Science, pp. 3-143.

25. Bjorneborn, L. (2004) Small-World Link Structures across an Academic workspace: a Library & Information Science Approach. Unpublished Doctoral dissertation, Royal Society of Library & Information Science Copenhagen, Denmark.

26. Bjorneborn, L., & Ingwersen, P. (2004) Towards a basic framework for Webometrics. Journal of American Society for Information Science & Technology. 55(14), 1216-1227.

27. Bjorneborn, Lennart (2008) Webometrics 2.0: Blogometrics, Wikimetrics, Tagometrics and Sociometrics revisted http://www.slideshare.net/Webometrics/webometrics20?src=related_normal&rel=546740

28. Gorkova, V.I. (1988) Informetrics, Informatics, 10. Moscow: VINITI.

29. Glanzel, W. (2003) Bibliometrics as a research field: a course on theory and application of bibliometric indicators. Course handouts online

at: http://scholar.google.com (Accessed on 12-02-2012).

30. Egghe, L. (2005) Expansion of the field of informetrics: Origins and Consequences, Information Processing & Management, 41, 1311-1316.

31. Björneborn , Lennart and Ingwersen, Peter. (2005). Toward a basic framework for webometrics.Journal of the American Society for Information Science and Technology, 55(14) 1216-1227.

32. Egghe, Leo and Rousseau, Ronald. (1990). Introduction to informetrics: Quantitative methods in library, documentation and information science. Amsterdam: Elsevier Science Publishers.

6
Information Systems

"Build a system that only a fool can use, and only a fool will want to use" — **George Bernard Shaw**

The word 'system' is derived from the latin word 'systema' and the greek word 'sutema' is an agglomerate of entity or objects, real or abstract comprising a whole where each and every component are related to each other. If any object does not inhibit any relationship with other element of the system then that object will not be an ingredient of the system.

For example, Human body system, solar system, transport system, education system etc.

System has been defined as an assemblage of procedures, processes, methods, routines, or technology united by some form of regulated interaction to form an organized whole. System has also been a subject of contentious issue among the scholars.

According to Ackoff and Emery (1972) system is a set of interrelated elements, each of which is related directly or indirectly to every other element and no subset of which is unrelated to any other subset.

Bertalanffy (1968) has attempted to derive a general definition of information as a complex of interacting component, concepts characteristics of organized wholes such as interaction, mechanization, centralization, competition etc to apply them to concrete phenomena.

On the other hand, K.M. Khailov (1968) applies the concept 'system' to biological entities. The theory unites the fundamental principles and encompasses most diverse natural, social and intellectual phenomenon.

An information system (IS) is typically considered to be a set of interrelated elements or components that collect (input), manipulate(processes), and disseminate (output) data and information and provide a feedback mechanism to meet an objective.

TYPES OF SYSTEM

Murdick and Ross Murdick,R.G. and Ross,J.E. Information system for modern management (Prentice-Hall,1975) have identified various systems. These include:

- **Conceptual system** : They are concerned with theoretical constructs.
- **Empirical system** : These are concrete functional system.
- **Natural system :** These are made by nature.
- **Man-made system :** These are result of human powered architect.
- **Social system :** It is made by people and includes inter-personal and group relationship.
- **Abstract system** : They are conceptual or non-physical entities.
- **Physical system :** They are tangible entities may be static or dynamic in operation.
- **Open system** : The system interacts freely with the environment.
- **Closed system** : They are self contained and does not

show any signs of influence of outside environment.

- **Stationary system :** Their properties and operations does not vary with time.
- **Non-stationary system :** These system vary with time.
- **Reactive system :** They interact with environment to improve function and adapt to the changing conditions.

SYSTEM THEORY

System theory is the transdisciplinary study of the abstract organization of phenomena, independent of their substance, type, or spatial or temporal scale of existence. It investigates both the principles common to all complex entities, and the (usually mathematical) models which can be used to describe them.

To understand system theory better one has to understand system approach, which mean a way of looking at a system from the point of view of interacting elements each directly influencing others i.e. in system approach one needs to translate the influence of each part to the whole in an interactive chain to determine those principles that describe and define these interactions. Another way, is to deal with specific systems and the principles governing their structure and function. It is concerned with categories of a system.

There are two forms of the theory:

(a) General System theory

In general system theory, one is not a part of system and judges that system from being outside the system. In general system theory one cannot know about the organization system. They are comparable, definable but cannot be explained. C.W. Churchman has referred to general system theory as a worldview.

For example, if one wants to know about Varanasi Ghats one can either read books or climb the topmost building and know about the same.

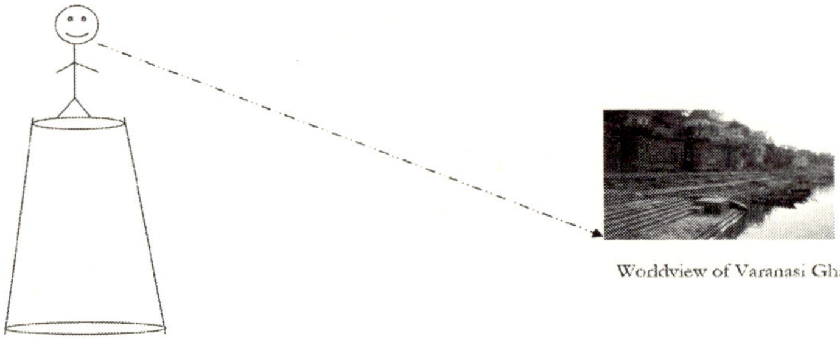

Worldview of Varanasi Ghats

(b) System theory

In system theory one is a part of system and judges it. One can evaluate the functions as well as its organs of the system.

For example, another way to know about the Varanasi Ghats is to visit each Ghats personally.

The analytical study carried out by Machlup and Mansfield (1983) has brought to notice certain issues for understanding a system. The conclusions of the study are:

1. There is no general agreement to the scope of systems theory.
2. System theory is primarily mathematical
3. System theory is not a theory of concrete system but a theory of models. It does not accept responsibility for the accuracy or relevance of these models.
4. System theory contribute to other sciences by generating a set of models for any well defined system but does not specify which model is best for a particular system.
5. System theory is reductionistic. Reductionism refers to attempts to isolate specific variables that influence a phenomenon for study.
6. System theory can provide the basis for organizing the social science.
7. While general system theory deals with the most fundamental, abstract or general aspects of system, system theory deals with more specific questions about more well-defined kinds of systems.

Development of information system

An information system is basically developed on the platform of information technology which is used to build information systems for various purposes. The conceptual framework of an information system is presented below:

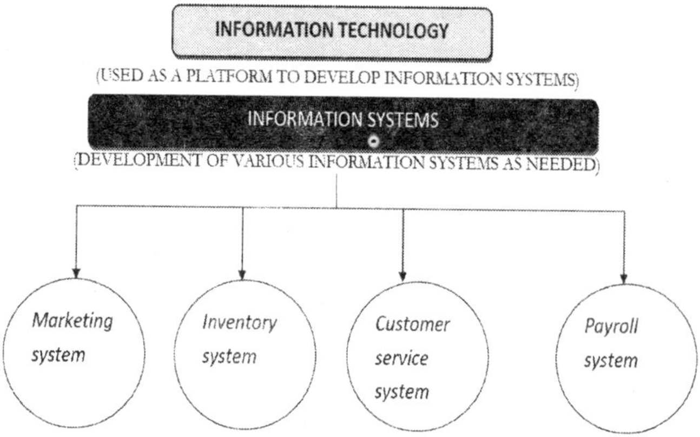

Features of information system

- They are composed of inter-related parts or sub-systems.
- They are hierarchical in nature
- Without affecting other parts , parts of a system cannot be changed
- Sub-systems cannot work independently
- All the components of a system work towards attaining a common goal
- All systems comprise of input, processes and outputs
- Sub-systems can belong to more than one systems

Categories of information system

Information systems can be broadly divided into two broad categories:

(a) Systems engaged in processing data generated by the organizations- Operating support system

(b) Systems employed to aid in decision making and management process- Management support system

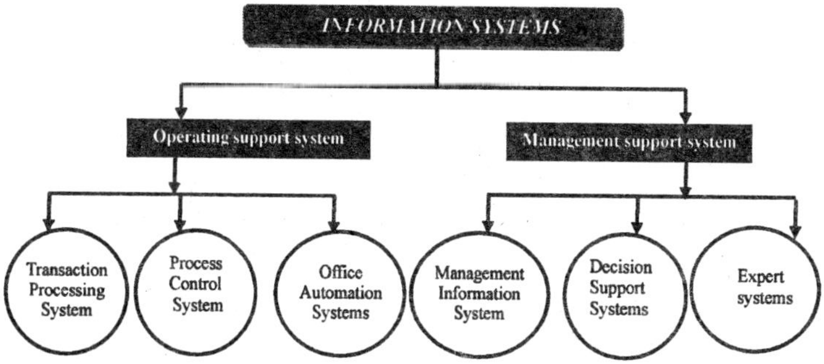

Transaction Processing System

It is a system which keeps track of the activities performed daily in an organization. They collect and store data relating to varied aspects of an organization, provide information necessary for day to day control of events and serve as the database for higher-level information systems.

Process Control System

They are used to monitor and control industrial processes

Office Automation Systems

These systems employ computers to automate many of the routine tasks that are performed in typical offices. It includes works like desktop publishing, electronic mail, FAX and image processing.

Management Information Systems

A management information system is a subset of the overall internal controls of a business covering the applications of people, documents, technologies and producers by management accountants to solve business problems such as costing a product, service or a business-wide strategy.

Management information systems are distinct from regular information systems in that they are used to analyze other information systems applied in operational activities in the organization. Management information systems are those systems that allow managers to make decision for the successful operation for businesses. The goal of the MIS organization is to deliver information to the various levels (top, middle, bottom) of corporate managers.

According to G.B. Davis, an MIS is an integrated user-machine system for providing information to support operations, management and decision making functions in an organization. The system utilizes computerized functions and manual procedures; models for analysis, planning, control and decision making; and a database.

Functions

1. To generate reports like financial statements, inventory status report, or performance reports needed for routine and non-routine purposes.
2. To answer what-if questions asked by management. For example "What would happen to cash flow if the company changes its credit term for its customers". This type of MIS can be called as simulation.
3. To aid in decision making

Characteristics

1. **Management oriented :** The system is designed from the top to work downwards. All the levels of management are provided with relevant information.
2. **Integration :** The word 'integration' means that system has to cover of all the functional areas of an organization so as to produce more meaningful management information, with a view to achieve the objectives of the organization.
3. **Heavy element :** A management information system cannot be established overnight. It takes 2 to 4 years to establish it successfully in an organization.
4. Flexibility and ease of use

Phases of development

Any system development requires four stages and so is for MIS:

- *Phase I : System planning* : initial problem is investigated.
- *Phase II:* Identification of the basic requirements of the systems like necessary hardware and software support.
- *Phase III: Development of system* : It involves designing and testing the system.
- *Phase IV : System implementation* : The newly made system is open for use and implementation. In this phase maintenance and evaluation of the system is done.

Planning for MIS

1. Identification of system requirements
2. Designing of MIS
3. Procurement of necessary material.
4. Installation of the system
5. Operation and follow up

Architecture of MIS

The component of a typical MIS has been plotted below:

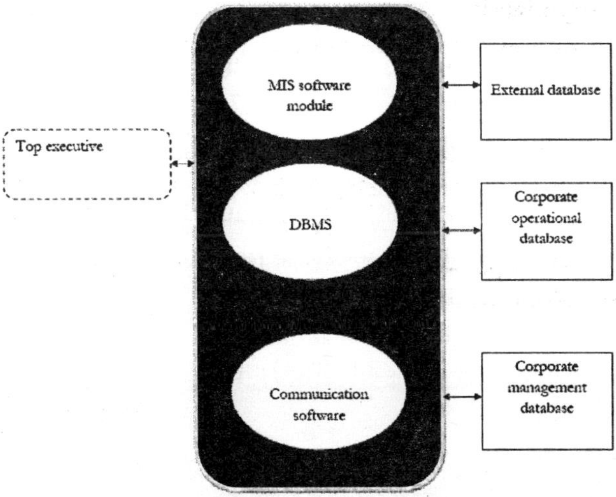

Types of MIS

There are five types of management information systems. It includes:

1. **Accounting management information systems :** All accounting reports are shared by all levels of accounting managers.
2. **Financial management information systems :** The chief financial officer analyzes historical and current financial activity, projects future financial needs and control the use of funds.
3. **Manufacturing management information systems :** Manufacturing operations continuously influenced by the changes or advances in technology. So this is handled by manufacturing MIS.
4. **Marketing management information systems :** A marketing management information system supports managerial activity in the area of product development, distribution, pricing decision, sales forecasting etc.
5. **Human resource management information systems:** They are concerned with the activities related to workers, managers and other individual employed by the organization. Activities include work-force analysis and planning, hiring, training and job assignments.

Operational hierarchy

An MIS activity encompasses varied activities of an organization like administration, marketing, production etc. These activities take place at several levels as shown below. Triangular shape has been used to show that each level is guided and controlled by the lower ones.

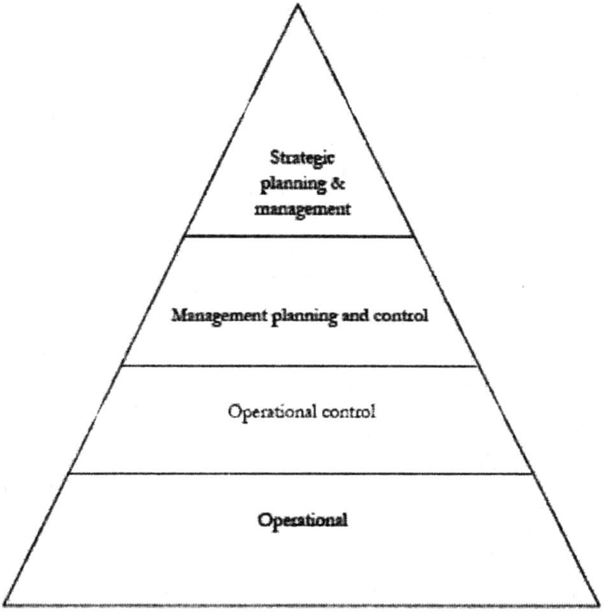

Nature of MIS

1. Report oriented
2. Action oriented
3. Expectation oriented
4. Database oriented
5. End-user oriented

Outputs of MIS

1. *Scheduled reports :* produced either periodically or on a schedule i.e. monthly, weekly or daily
2. *Demand reports :* gives information at mangers request
3. *Key-indicator reports :* available at the beginning of the day
4. *Exception reports :* produced during unusual or management action.

Benefits

1. *It helps increase competitiveness* : MIS provides tools necessary to gain a better understanding of enterprise and its objectives.
2. *Enhance supply chain management*: Improved reporting improves the management of the supply chain including manufacturing to distribution of finished products.
3. *Quick reflexes* : MIS systems enable an enterprise move quickly to their environment, enabling them to push out ahead of the competition.

Need of implementation of MIS in libraries

- To maintain better accountability and control of resources
- To monitor budget allocations
- To improve overall library effectiveness by focusing on outcomes
- To generate internal and external reports
- To improve long term planning
- To facilitate performance measure activities

Despite its benefits of processing voluminous data, the serious drawback is the human intervention, the data processed are ultimately feed in by the human being and therefore there is a chance of error and bias. But, even then the usefulness of an MIS cannot be neglected and testimony is its increasing use in organizations.

DECISION SUPPORT SYSTEMS

Decision support system is an interactive, user-friendly management level computer system that combines data and sophisticated analytical models and tools to support semi-structured and unstructured decision making. A DSS does not make decisions rather it is a powerful tool that is used to support decision-making. They are potent tools for decision taking through scientific methods and techniques developed by information science. Human judgment and decision making is affected drastically in complex matters and stress conditions.

Turban Turban, E. Decision support and expert systems, Managerial perspectives, Macmillan, 1988 defines decision support system as 'interactive computer-based systems that help decision makers to utilize data and models to solve relatively unstructured problems'.

According to Druzdzel, Marek J. and Flynn, Roger R. 'Decision support systems', Encyclopedia of Library and Information Sciences, Taylor and Francis, 2010 disciplines such as statistics, economics and operations research developed various methods of making rational choices. These methods have enhanced by various techniques originating from information science, cognitive psychology, and artificial intelligence, have been implemented in the form of computer programs, either as a stand-alone tools or as an integrated computing environments for complex decision making.

Characteristics

Alter (1980) has put forth three major characteristics of DSS:

- They are designed to facilitate decision processes
- They should support rather than automate decision making
- They should be able to respond quickly to the changing needs of decision makers.

Another set of characteristics are:

- It should facilitate and aid in decision making
- It should be designed for interactive use
- It should support decision makers at any level of organization
- They are intended for repeated use.
- It should have capability to support one or more tasks

- It should be an integrated information system.

Components of DSS

Sage, A.P. in Decision Support Systems Engineering; John Wiey and Sons, Inc.: New York,1991 has listed three fundamental components:

Database Management System (DBMS) : A DBMS serves as a data bank for the DSS. It stores large quantities of data that are relevant to the class of problems for which the DSS has been designed and provides logical data structures (as opposed to the physical data structures) with which the users interact. A DBMS separates the users from the physical aspects of the database structure and processing. It should also be capable of informing the user of the types of data that are available and how to gain access to them.

Model base Management System (MBMS) : The role of MBMS is analogous to that of a DBMS. Its primary function is providing independence between specific models that are used in a DSS from the applications that use them. The purpose of an MBMS is to transform data from the DBMS into information that is useful in decision making. Since many problems that the user of a DSS will cope with may be unstructured, the MBMS should also be capable of assisting the user in model building.

Dialog Generation and Management System (DGMS): The main product of an interaction with a DSS is insight. As their users are often managers who are not computer-trained, DSSs need to be equipped with intuitive and easy-to-use interfaces. These interfaces aid in model building, but also in interaction with the model, such as gaining insight and recommendations from it. The primary responsibility of a DGMS is to enhance the ability of the system user to utilize and benefit from the DSS. In the remainder of this article, we will use the broader term user interface rather than DGMS.

User : Architecture of DSS:

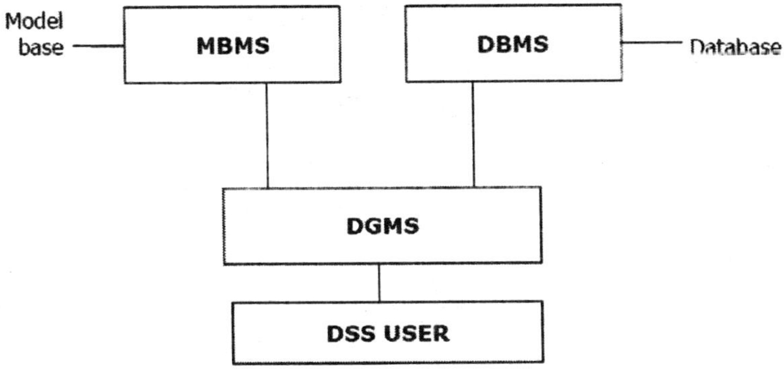

DSS MODELS

There are three models of DSS:

Passive DSS : Decision support systems that just collect data and organize it effectively are usually called passive models, they do not suggest a specific decision, and they only reveal the data.

Active DSS : An active decision support system actually processes data and explicitly shows solutions based upon that data.

Cooperative DSS : A cooperative decision support system is when data is collected, analyzed and then is provided to a human component which then can help the system revise or refine it. It means that both a human component and computer component work together to come up with the best solution.

Architecture of DSS

The conceptual schema of a DSS is as below:

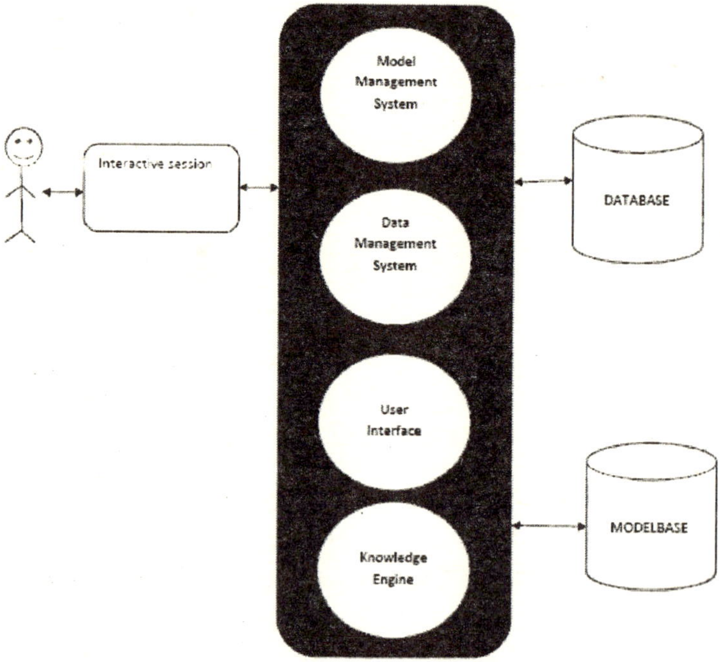

Benefits

Potential benefits of using DSS are:

- Augments the decision maker's own innate knowledge management abilities
- It can solve problems that a decision maker alone can not do
- It provides speedy and reliable solutions
- Stimulates the decision maker's thought about the problem.
- Provides sound base to justify decision maker's position.
- Contributes to an organization's competitiveness.

Implications of DSS

- Clinical Decision Support System for medical diagnosis
- In Banking, verifying the credit of loan applicant

- Extensively used in business and management
- In agricultural production, marketing for sustainablc development
- In railways
- Stock market

EXPERT SYSTEM

An expert system is a system designed for solving problems in a particular application area. One can draw inference from a stored knowledge base that is developed by recording and structuring human expertise through an individual called a knowledge engineer. It is an information system that captures the knowledge or expertise of a specialist and then simulates the thinking of that expert for those with less or no experience. They are also referred as knowledge based systems or artificial intelligence based systems. According to Schwartz an Expert System is a computer programmes that simulates the reasoning process that a human being would go through in performing a particular task.

Traits of ES

1. Captures knowledge and expertise of a problem solver or decision maker
2. Simulates the thinking of those with less knowledge
3. It has narrow domain of knowledge
4. It has capability to reason and explain
5. The interaction is from machine to the user.
6. It acts as a consultant to the user
7. The Expert System is always available and instant;
8. Skills of several experts can be combined;
9. It is logical, objective and consistent;
10. It does not forget or make mistakes in calculations;
11. It is directly and instantly available for consultation;

12. Access is not limited by time and location;
13. It is useful in training programmes ;
14. When faced with an unusual situation-human expert develop entirely new, original approaches.

Branchman has also put forth various characteristics that are fundamental to an expert system

1. Expertise
2. Symbol manipulation
3. Intelligence
4. Complexity
5. Reformulation
6. Reasoning about self
7. Type of task

Need for expert systems

i. Human experts may retire, join another firm;
ii. Human experts can only be in one place at one time;
iii. Human experts require considerable time in training;
iv. They are difficulties to interact with human experts; and
v. Human experts may be emotion bound, forgetful.

Henceforth, there is a need to design expert systems to have a sound and uninterrupted think-tank.

Kinds of expert systems

Broadly there are four categories of expert systems:

- Advice systems
- Decision-support systems
- Intelligent interfaces
- Learning systems

Components of an expert system

- **The knowledge base :** It stores all the facts and rules about a particular problem domain. It makes these available to the inference engine in a form that it can use.

- **The Inference engine or shell :** It is the programs that locates the appropriate knowledge in the knowledge base, and infers new knowledge by applying logical processing and problem-solving strategies.
- **The User Interface :** It is the means of communication between a user and the expert systems problem-solving processes.

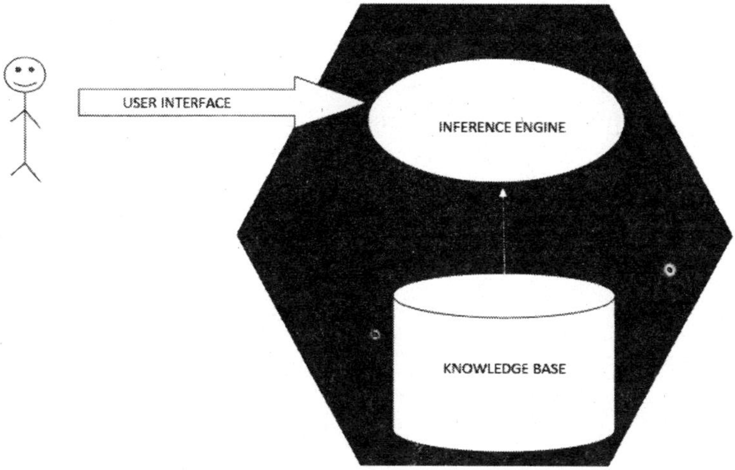

EXPERT SYSTEM

Workflow in expert systems

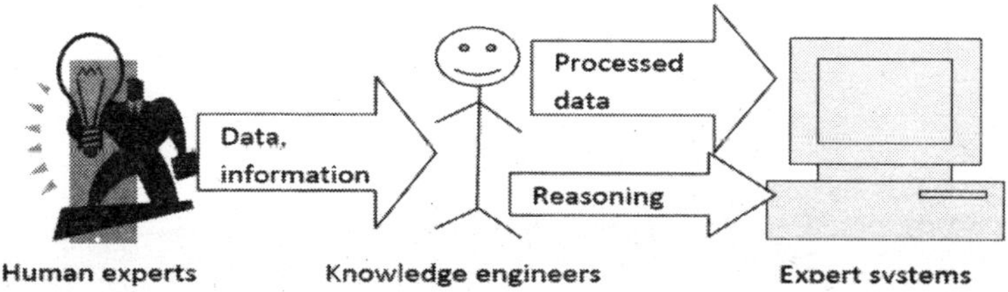

Languages of expert systems

- List Processing Language:- LISP
- Logic Programming Language:-PROLOG
- Object Oriented Language:- SMALL TALK
- Conventional Programming Language:-PASCAL, FORTRAN, C, BASIC

Applications

- Industrial applications
- Financial applications
- Social applications
- Global news agencies like; Reuter, CNN have to handle huge news reports. They have developed Topic Identifications Systems.

Implications in Libraries

- In Cataloguing
  - — Prototype expert cataloguing system
  - — AutoCat Prototype
  - — Prototype Expert System MAPPER
  - — Catalyst
  - — MITINET
- In Reference Service
  - — Answerman
  - — POINTER
  - — COMIT
- In Referral Service
  - — PLEXUS
- For Online Search
  - — TOMSEARCH

Advantages

- Combines knowledge of many experts in a specific fields
- Stores unlimited amount of information
- Available 24 hours a day
- Can be used at distance over a network

Limitations

- They are rule based systems.
- They work in restricted domain
- Expertise needs to be gathered and codified which is in the form of facts and rules; and
- They work on principle of knowledge base, user interface and inference mechanism.

Real life example

Windows operating system trouble shooting

REFERENCES

1. Ackoff, R.L. (1967) Management misinformation systems. Management science 14(4), 18-20
2. Head, R.V. (1970) Elusive MIS Datamation 16(10),22
3. Argyris, C. Management information systems: the challenge for rationality and emotionality. Management science 17)6), B275-B292
4. Zani, W.M. Blueprint for MIS. Harvard Business Review 48(6), 95
5. Alter, S.L. (1977) Taxonomy of Decision Support Ststem. Sloan Management Review. 19; Fall. Pp. 39-56
6. Bonczek, Robert H. et. al. (1981) Foundation of decision support system. New York: Academic Press, pp. 11-13.
7. Ginzberg, Michael J. and Stohr, Eduerd A (1982) Decision Support System: Issues and perspectives In Ginzber, M.J. and Reitman, W ed: New York: Elseivier
8. Holsapple, C.W. (1995) Decision support systems: a knowledge based approach, St Paul, MN: West Publishing Company
9. Keen, P.G.W. and Scott Morton, M.S. (1978) Decision support systems: an organizational perspectives. Reading, MA: Addison-Welsley

10. Simon, H.A. (1960) The new science of management decision. New York: Harper & Row
11. George, J.F. (1991) The conceptualization and development of organizational decision support systems. Journal of Managemnt information systems, Vol. 8, No. 3
12. Dennis, A. and Wixom, B.H. (2000) System analysis and design. New York: Wiley
13. Gill, T.G. The early expert systems. What are they now? MIS Quarterly, Vol. 19, no.1
14. Choudhary, G.G. (2005) Introduction of modern information retrieval. London: Facet
15. Zahedi, F. (1999) Intelligent system for business. Belmont, CA:Wadsworth
16. Holtzman, S. (1995) Intelligent decision systems; Adison-Wesley:Reading,MA
17. Sprague, R and Watson H. (1986) Decision support systems: putting theory into practice, Prentice-Hall
18. Turban, E. (1988) Decision support and expert systems: Managerial perspectives, Macmillan
19. Raskin, J. (2000) The human interface: new directions for designing interactive systems, Addison-Wesley
20. Dubey, Yogendra P. Decision support system:development and trends In Encyclopaedia of computer science and technology. Vol. 19, Allen kent & James William, ed New York: Marcel Dekker.

7

Information Societies

"In the information society, nobody thinks. We expect to banish paper, but we actually banish thought."

—Michael Crichton

Information is indicative of certain attributes of society where information serves as a crucial role in transforming the behavior of society. It differs from the primitive societies in terms of quality as well as accessibility to information. With the infestation of information and communication technology the very concept of information has underwent a phenomenal change. Society on the other side represents the collectivity of human kinship. As an allied concept one may visualize information society as a society where information and its associated phenomena gain prodigious significance. Commenting on the emergence of information society Masuda opines that making of information values became the formative forces for the development of information based society. Also, Nick Moore in The Information Society argues that the origin and causes of information socicties lie in two interrelated developments: long term economic development and technological change. In other words information society refers to such a society where information serves as a socio-economic and cultural motor. Due to decline in traditional industries like mining and metallurgy, there evolved an increasing focus on the intangible product of human intellect i.e. information leading to an information based economy.

The term "information society" was firstly used in early 1960s in Japanese social science. The Japanese version of expression (joho shakai, johoka shakai) sprouted in 1961which was reported to the people in written texts as a title of study in 1964.

Defining an information based society has been a contested project among the savants. In lack of agreement of interpretations it is fair to have a cursory look on the views put forth by the prominent scholars.

Daniel Bell defines it as a society that organizes itself around knowledge in the interest of social control, and the management of innovation and change. On the other hand, Yoneji Masuda opines that information society represents a new type of society where the possession of information and not material wealth is the driving force behind its transformation and development and where intellectual creativity flourishes. While, John Naisbitt argues that the information society is an economic reality and not simply a mental abstraction. The slow spread / dissemination of information ends new activities, operations and products gradually come to light. Further, Nick Moore has opined that a society where information is used as an economic resource, the community harnesses or exploits it, and behind it all an industry develops which produces the necessary information is referred as information society. Similarly, Bela Muranyi has argued that information society connotes a new type of society in which humanity has the opportunity to lead a new way of life, to have a higher standard of living, accomplish better work, and to play a better role in society thanks to the global use of information and telecommunication technologies.

Factors that precipitated the need of an information society

1) Advancement of information and communication technology.
2) Decentralization of computers reducing the monopoly of institutions and cyber cafes.
3) Concurrence of information and communications media.
4) Development of information industries.
5) Transition from industrial economy to an information economy.
6) Large volume of services based on electronic infrastructure.
7) Development of information services based on telecommunication infrastructure.
8) Optimal usage of IT in every aspects

Transition to Information society

Change is the essence of any society. The emergence of an information society was characterized by three major epochs of history:

Agrarian society

Industrial society

Information society

In the book "The third wave", Toffler describes three types of societies, based on the concept of 'waves', each wave pushes the older societies and cultures aside.

- **First Wave** is the society after agrarian revolution and replaced the first hunter-gatherer cultures.
- **The Second Wave** Society is industrial and based on mass production, mass distribution, mass consumption, mass

education, mass media, mass recreation, mass entertainment, and weapons of mass destruction.

- **Third Wave** is the post-industrial society. He added that during 1950s most of the second wave countries were moving to the third wave.He coined many words to describe it and mentions names invented by others, such as the Information Age.

This transition was not sudden rather the product of long term evolution process. The evolution of information society can be viewed from three dimensions – historical, economic and political.

Historical dimension
(Journey from handwritten to printed)

Origin of writing
↓
Use of alphabets
↓
Visual representation of objects and shapes
↓
Use of rocks, bones or wood for recording
↓
Development of book
↓
Development of printing leading to revolution in communication
↓
Development of book trade
↓
Development of new techniques for printing pictorial image
↓
Development of techniques for recording and transmission of sound
↓
Development of wireless broadcasting (radio, television and cinema)
↓
Development of computers
↓
Use of internet leading to a virtual world

Economic dimension (Emergence of information markets)

Agrarian economy
↓
Industrial economy
↓
Information economy

Political dimension

Realization of the value of information
↓
Monopoly of information rich countries over information
↓
Divides the world into information rich and poor
↓
Changes in information delivery systems with internet and computers
↓
Digital divide in world
↓
Initiatives by the government and leaders leading to availability of digital media
↓
Threats to information capital (plagiarism, piracy)
↓
Need to protect intellectual property
↓
Development of Intellectual Property rights (copyright, Censorship)
↓
Development of copy left (freedom to information)

Features of an information society

1) Information and telecommunication technologies play significant role in social subsistence
2) Domination of information sectors and information oriented jobs.
3) Reduced physical distance
4) Influence of digital media to our culture, lifestyle and society.
5) Connectivity to a virtual world through networks

6) Information is used as an economic resource

7) Large usage of information to increase an organization's efficiency and competitive hold.

8) Use of information to exert civil rights by citizens

Yoneji Masuda in Information society as Post- Industrial Society has laid down the characteristics of an information society:

Innovational technology	Core	Computer
	Basic function	Amplification of mental labor
	Productive power	Information productive power
Socio-economic structure	Products	Information, technology
	Production centre	Information Industries
	Market	Information space
	Leading industries	Information & Knowledge industries
	Industrial structure	Matrix structure
	Economic structure	Synergetic economy
	Socio-economic principle	Law of goals
	Socio-economic subject	Voluntary communities
	Socio-economic system	Infrastructure principle
	Form of society	Functional society
	National goal	Gross National Satisfaction
	Form of government	Participatory democracy
	Force of social change	Citizen's movement, litigation
	Social problems	Future shock, terror, piracy
	Most advanced stage	High mass knowledge creation
Values	Value standards	Time value
	Ethical standards	Social contribution
	Spirit of the times	Symbiosis of man and nature

Components of an information society

Schement and Curtis in "Tendencies and tensions of the

information age: the production and distribution of information in United States" has laid down six elemental constituents of information society. These are:

Information commodities

Market-and commercial processes related to their production.

Information industry

Industries built on the large scale manufacturing, production, distribution and consumption of information in an increasingly global competitive arena, where information export is the measure of the economic fitness.

Information work

It represents the shift of traditional employment indicators towards employers and professions dealing with information.

Interconnectedness

It implies that increasing social complexity and labour distribution are realized through increasingly indispensable technological support through increasingly indispensable technological support systems, while technology facilitates the emergence of secondary networks in addition to the traditional (primary) ones.

Parallel use of several media

It is the cohesive power of communities of increasing size, independent of the debates surrounding the dysfunctions of the new media.

Interaction of technological and social progress

Strengthening of new community formulae versus traditional (economic, scientific and political elites.

IMPLICATIONS OF INFORMATION ON SOCIETY

Information is having very significant explications on society. Today's society cannot run without the free flow of information. It is characterized by:

1. Pervasive influence of information on home, work and recreational aspects of individuals
2. Stratification of society into new classes, those who are information rich and those who are information poor.

Apart from the above points, it is very important to mention Alvin Toffler's "Future shock" in which he surmised how the pace of evolution has increased due to free flow of information and how it is affecting society.

In his other work "Third wave" he suggests that after the agricultural revolution and industrial revolution, it is the information revolution that is taking place.

Furthermore, information is influencing every aspect of society:

Government

Government is the greatest generator and consumers of information in modern times. All government activities start with information and end with generation of more information.

In modern times, government generates a large amount of data for national planning, preparing a large amount of data for national planning, preparing alternate strategies and models for development.

In India, National Informatics Centre Network (NICNET) provides a computer based information system to the various government departments to access a variety of information.

Agriculture

Information is very much important for sustainable agriculture and this is the reason why "choupal" and "e-choupal" are organized by the governments to disseminate information of importance related to agriculture.

Various information systems (like AGRIS) and kiosks has also been set up by the government to improve the agricultural productivity.

Buisness & Industry

Business and industry were first to use the techniques of management information system to process and provide information on markets, regulation on trade and tariffs etc as they are invaluable if an enterprise has to thrive.

Basically there are three kinds of information requirements of industries:

- Information regarding raw sources
- Production related information
- Marketing related information

Daily Life of Individuals

An ordinary person in his daily life is heavily dependent on information like food, health care, education and entertainment, social security.

It is the above needs that have forced the areas like e-learning and telemedicine to emerge. Also, the information system of railways cannot be left to mention.

So the information is leading a complete transformation of society.

World Summit on the Information Society

The world summit on the information society (WSIS) was a pair of UN-sponsored conferences about information, communication and in broad terms the information society that took place in 2003 in Geneva and in 2005 in Tunis. The main aim of the summit was to bridge the digital divide separating rich countries from poor countries by separating access to the internet in the developing world. Every year 17th May is observed as world information society day.

Emanating Information Industries

The most exemplifying streak of information society is the emanation or development of information industry. The information industry comprises a group of enterprises and organizations whose purpose is to produce and process information and to develop the infrastructure and delivery mechanisms to distribute information. Most of the countries have realized the potential of intellectual wealth and are now actively engaged in the creation of indigenous information industries to keep pace with the expanding international information marketplace.

Structure of Industries

The functions of the information can be primarily divided into four categories: Production, Processing, Distribution and the building of an infrastructure. Additionally, manufacturing of information processing tool and research development industry also comes under its purview.

Production

This category of information industry produces and sells information. For example, companies specializing in data mining use large collection of data to create usable information products such as customer profiles or product purchasing trends. Newspaper, Electronic media, movies and publishing etc. are also included in production of information. They are the direct sellers of information.

Processing

Information processing comprises a large portion of activities within the information industry; processing transforms information into products that can be packaged and sold as a usable goods:

For example, publishing a journal involves processing a member of articles into an edited and integrated package.

Creating electronic databases of journal articles involves assembling citations and abstracts for articles from a carefully selected group of journals and encouraging into a usable database system. Its examples are ISI web knowledge, SCOPUS, and EBSCO databases

Distribution / Dissemination

Distribution of information also comprises a large part of industrial activity, distribution includes marketing the information products that were processed and delivering the products to the customers who purchase them.

For example, once an electronic database of journal articles has been assembled, proper distribution ensures that potential customers know it exists and they can access it after purchase. Search engines, telecommunication and broadcasting also comes under this category of information industry

Infrastructure

Finally, information industry organizations must build a robust infrastructure in order to support their activities. Such an infrastructure may include for example computer hardware and software, database systems, telecommunication systems, marketing channels and other technological and social structures.

Additionally there are two categories also:

Manufacturing of information processing tool

Broadcasting instrument etc.

Research-development industry

All organizations use information for research and development purpose for e.g. Intel etc. Ergonomics is heavily influenced by this category.

All these activities of the information industry do not operate in vacuum. The information industry includes people like knowledge mangers, information technology mangers.

Finally, the information industry is in a state of flux in which the only guarantee is constant change.

The structure of information industries has been a contested project leading to diversifying conflicting interpretations. In dilemma to select a single typology, it is fair to have a cursory look on the significant ones.

Libby Trudell in How to Understand and Influence the Information Industry has laid five functional information based industries:

1. Primary publishers : These organizations are responsible for publishing the primary literature in serial or monograph form. They add quality by selecting the informative and new articles, identifying appropriate authors, providing editorial oversight and control, through peer reviews, and skillfully marketing and promoting their publications. Previously, the primary publishers were engaged in production of print media, but that is changing rapidly with new providers for e- books and e-journals as well as web-enabled social media.

Some of the key publishers of scientific journal literature include

- Elsevier
- Blackwell
- Wolters Kluwer
- Springer-Verlag, plus

2. Secondary publishers : These publishers provide better accessibility to primary publications by indexing and abstracting the primary publications. To a great extent they depend on the cooperation with the primary publishers in order to have access to the source material, or may work directly with other types of source publications such as patents and trademarks. Initially published in print form, such indexes are now available mostly as databases in electronic format. Many secondary publishers offer access to their own database(s) via their website.

Examples of scientific and technical abstract and indexing providers are:

- Thomson
- Scientific
- Biosis
- Derwent World Patent Index
- ISI Science Citation Index
- Medline

3. Online services and solutions : Online services are distribution channels for both secondary and primary publishers. They add value by aggregating many secondary and primary sources into a single environment, usually with a powerful search engine, and bundling in specialized capabilities for information delivery, formatting, analysis and customization. These services are evolving themselves to adapt to the changing user needs and keep pace with time.

Examples of online services are:

- Dialog
- LexisNexis
- STN
- Ovid

4. Software and solutions providers : With all this data flowing into the organization, librarians and information professionals need tools for managing, organizing and providing access to it through internal systems and to clients' desktops. This is a rapidly changing arena, with a number of open source options available as well as major commercial players.

A wide range of software providers operate in this space like:

- enterprise database management tools such as Oracle and SAP
- content or document management systems such as

Autonomy and Open Text

- intranet portal tools such as BEA's Plumtree.

5. Library Technical Services : Another category of service suppliers are those who help run the library's "back room," providing tools for cataloging, circulation and public access. These library automation services are commonly referred to as integrated library systems (ILS) or Online Public Access Catalogs (OPACs). The largest player in shared cataloging is OCLC, a non-profit membership organization with more than 57,000 participating libraries worldwide. However, there are many options for stand-alone software and solutions providers like:

- EOS
- Sirsi-Dynix
- ExLibris
- Innovative Interfaces.

Nick Moore in **The information society** has divided the information sector into three distinct segments: the first concerned with the creation of information- the content sector, the second concerned with the delivery of the information; and the third concerned with information processing.

I. Information-content industry : It consists of public and private sector organizations which are accountable for the production and development of the intellectual property.

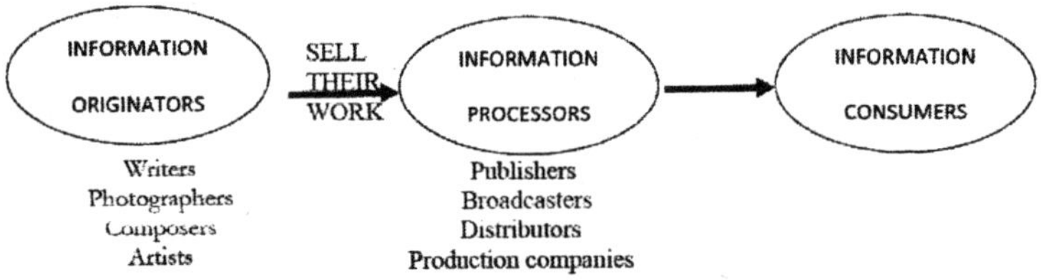

II. Information- delivery industry : These are the channels or networks through which information is communicated. Some of the channels are:

- Telecommunication companies
- Cable-television networks
- Satellite broadcasters
- Cellular telecommunication companies
- Radio and television stations
- Booksellers
- Libraries
- Value-added network services

III. Information-processing industry : These industries are dedicated to the cause of processing of information. They can be divided into two parts:

(a) **Hardware producers :** They design, develop, manufacture and market computers, telecommunications equipment and consumer electronics

(b) **Software producers :** They provide us with operating systems like LINUX, DOS or Windows applications packages like spreadsheets and word processors

EMERGING INFORMATION PROFESSION

The information needs of the governments, institutions, businesses, and individuals can at its level best be satisfied only if it matches with the available resources and the same is made available to the potential users. To match with the quality of service the traditional library profession has shifted to information profession as their work is completely different from their traditional counterparts. Information profession has emerged as an intermediary between the information sources, information systems and information users.

Profession can be defined as the occupation one does for the purpose of livelihood. It is also known as job, line of work, position, business etc. Any profession usually requires an academic degree. Information profession as a profession has been subjected to contestation of ideas leading to three schools of thoughts:

I. Information profession is not a profession supported by Madden, Moon, Moore and Mc Pheron

II. Information profession is an emerging profession argued by Goode, Rossi, Shaffer and Gullis

III. Information profession is a full-fledged profession supported by Dewey, Bundy, Reeves and Aishen

Lack of any consensus of opinions among the scholars forces us to see the core attributes that a profession should inhibit. These are:

- Body of specialized knowledge and technical skills
- Formal training and experience
- Ethical code or standard of conduct
- Commitment to public service rather than monetary gain
- As a course of curriculum or study
- Financial return should not be the measure of success
- Separatism
- Professional associations

Since all the aforesaid parameters are followed by the information profession it can be considered as a field of professional practice.

International Encyclopedia of Information and Library Science (Routledge, 2003) has put forth three elements essential to information profession. These are:

- Engagement in the provision of information services using a collection of information developed for a community of users.
- Responsibility for the construction, management and movement of information from one situation or place to another
- Professional decisions about information policy and design for collecting, holding and providing the information.

Information professional

An information professional is an individual who has obtained a professional degree and has some specialization over the profession. Some of the areas where information professionals are required are:

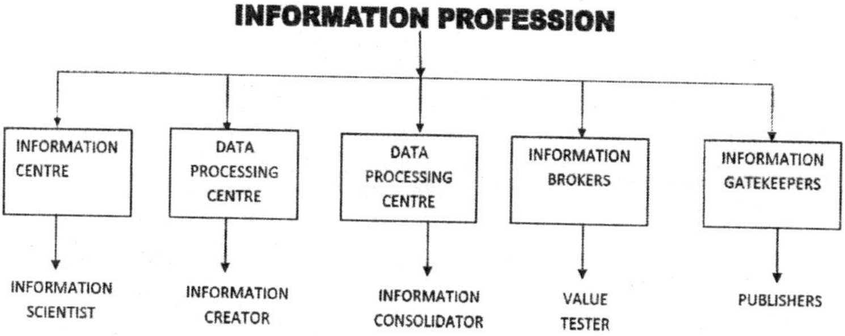

With the above categorization of information profession, we can certainly say that the role of libraries has changed. From libraries we are moving towards the concepts like virtual libraries i.e. the library without walls where information specialists will categorize the documents. There are information centres where the information scientist acts as the professional. Similarly, there are data processing centre and data consolidation centres wherein information creator and information consolidator works as a professional.

Besides, there are newly emerging destinations like information broker who judges the value of information; also information gatekeepers who controls the passage of information. Publishers come under the purview of last category. The library and information professional may be changing but the seven lamps of professional ethics are still the same as given by R.L. Mittal. They are:

1. Impersonal book selection
2. Service before self
3. Split-mind

4. Sympathetic behaviour
5. Tact
6. Laborious
7. Scholarship

Although, the nature of information profession is changing with the flow of fast and new information every day; it is in the interest of library professional and the information scientist to keep them abreast of nascent information.

Core values of information profession

The foundation of information profession rests on essential set of core values which define, guide, and inform all professional practices. These values reflect the history and ongoing developments of the profession and have been advanced, expanded and refined by a numerous policy statements of ALA. Among these are:

- Access
- Privacy
- Democracy
- Diversity
- Education and life-long learning
- Intellectual freedom
- Preservation
- The Public good
- Professionalism
- Service
- Social responsibility

Development of information profession

The development of information profession is not a sudden development rather the product of long term evolution adapting to the changing focus areas and influence of information technologies.

Different phases of development are:

- 1876- Library economy
- 1900- Librarianship
- 1950- Library & Information Science
- 2000- Information Science

According to Girja Kumar library and information science profession passed through three epochs of evolution of the profession.

- 1876-1950 (Descriptive era) Practical librarianship
- 1950-2000 (Dynamism era) Need of establishing theory
- 2000-till date (Digital era) Emergence of digital libraries.

Role of information professionals in the 21st century

1) With the internet, the librarian's job of sorting and providing access has become even greater.
2) Manage the consequences of digital revolution like bibliographic databases, digital catalogues, use of barcodes
3) Given the plethora of information available the internet has heightened the need for more and better librarians for information filtering
4) Employing and using RSS feeds to stream current information
5) Need to impart user education.

REFERENCES

1. Webster, Frank (2004) The information society reader. London: Routledge
2. Hundley, Richard ... [et al.] (2003) The global course of information revolution: recurring themes and regional variations. Santa Monica, CA: Rand
3. Martin William J. (1995) The global information society. UK: Aslib Gower
4. Trend, David. (2001) Reading digital cultures. London: Blackwell Publishers

5. Robertson, Douglas (1998) The new renaissance: computers and the next level of civilization. UK: Oxford

6. Lyon, David (1995) The roots of the information society idea. Information technology and society: a reader. London: Sage

7. Alistair, Duff S. ...[et al.] (1996) A note on the origin of the information society. Journal of information science. 22

8. Burton, Paul (1992) Information technology and society: implications for the information professions. London: LA publishing.

9. Abott, Andrew (1991) The order of professionalization, work and occupations 18 (Nov. 19): 355-384

10. Feather, John (2000) The information society: a study of continuity and change. London: LA publishing

11. Meadows, A. J. (ed.) (1995) Knowledge and communication: essays on the information chain. London: LA publishing

12. Hill, Michael W. (1999) The impact of information on society. London: Bowkar-Sour

13. Hayward, W. (1995) Information rich, Information poor: access and excahage in global society. London: Bowkar-Sour

14. Munsinghae, Mohan (ed.) Computers and informatics in developing countries. London: Butterworth.

15. Rubin, Richard E. (2004) Foundations of library and information science. New York: Neal-Schuman

16. Trudell ,Libby (2007) How to Understand and Influence the Information Industry (*www.eprints.rclis.org*) Accessed on 12 Jan 2012.

8

Information Sources on the Web

"Information is a source of learning. But unless it is organized, processed, and available to the right people in a format for decision making, it is a burden, not a benefit"

— William Polard

The World Wide Web has evolved as an important or popular source of information in digital revolution. The onset of information age has paved the way for information society. The user approach to information seeking has undergone a drastic change that prefers e-resources than going to library and scans the print sources. Libraries being a socio-centric institution have to meet up with times to justify its existence and to keep pace with times. Web has been a nodal point of revolution from information generation to its access and usage to retrieval. In the web environment there is need for the librarians to master the art of information searching and literacy. In order to tame the mammoth digital information librarians need to act as a facilitator.

Types of web-resources

Web resources can be grouped into four elemental categories: (K.Thulasi, NCSI www.ncsi.iisc.ernet.in/raja/netlis/iirml/kt1.ppt)

1. Primary sources

Conference proceedings : Conference proceedings in academic fields are the amassment of academic papers that are published relating to an academic conference. They are published to inform a wider audience of the papers presented at the conference. They are pivotal tool for the cutting-edge developments in a field. Further conferences being a standard tool for information sharing entire scientific community does not attend it for which the publication of conference proceedings are an exemplary solutions.

Example :

(a) Conference proceedings of offshore wind energy projects

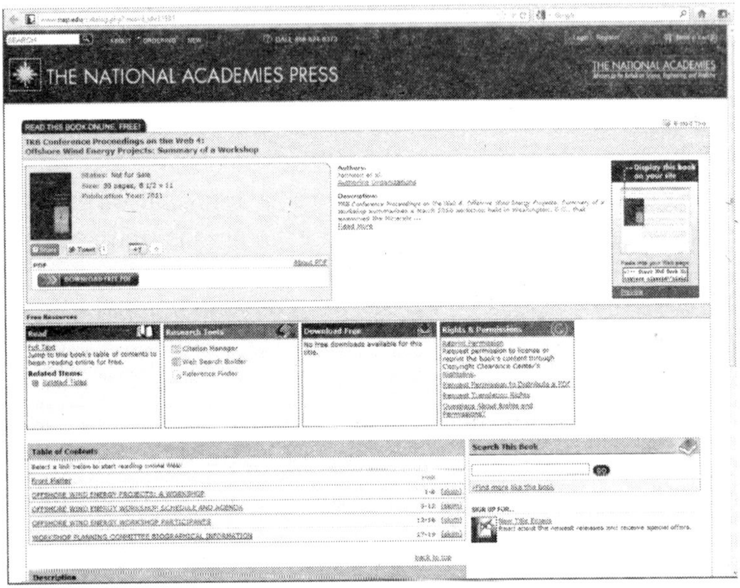

(b) Conference proceedings citation index of ISI

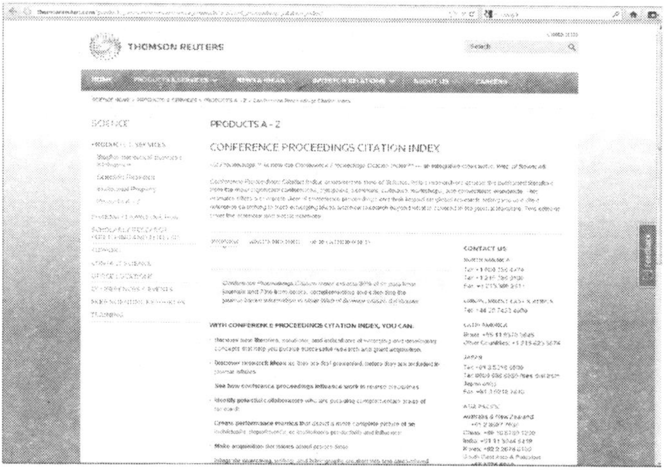

Courseware/ tutorials/ slides/ manuals : They are power point slides of course or other topics for exploiting and bringing interest of the people through visuals. There are plenty of sources on the web that provides access to presentations or tutorials that can be accessed as well as downloaded online.

Example:

i. Slides, course materials and tutorials on slide share

ii. Articles, books and presentations on scribd

E-journals : They are the scholarly carriers of intellectual productivity via electronic means. They are published on the web based platforms. They are of two types: open source (freely available) and closed source (available on some charge or on subscription basis)

Example :

1. Open access online journals available through Jstor.

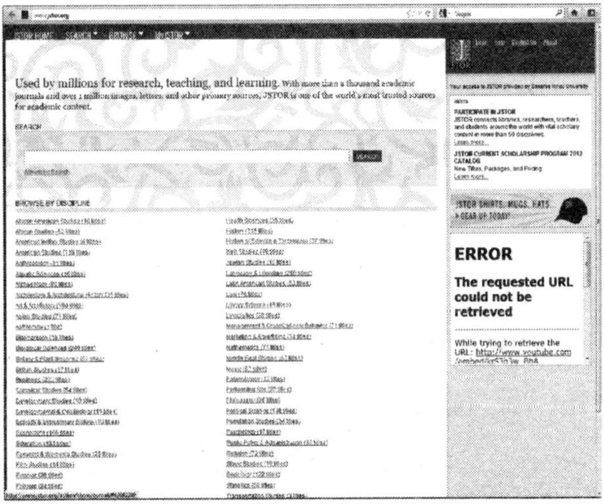

2. Closed access online journals available through Sage

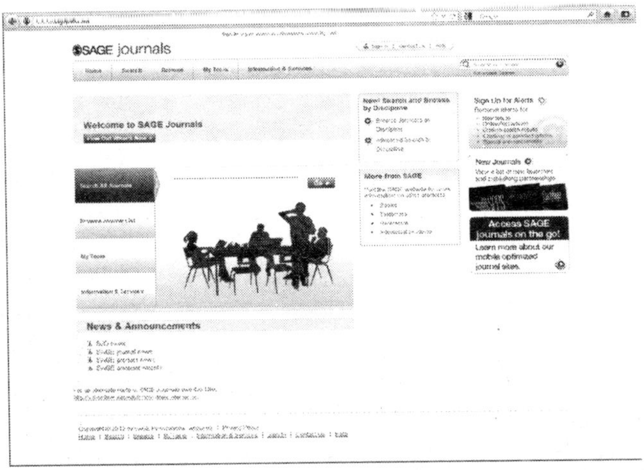

Patents : They are the exclusive rights granted to an inventor regarding his or her monopoly over the product. It is very handy tool as the inventors can scan through the patent databases or indexes being trying to get his or her works patentable.

Example:

a. Derwent patent index available through STN

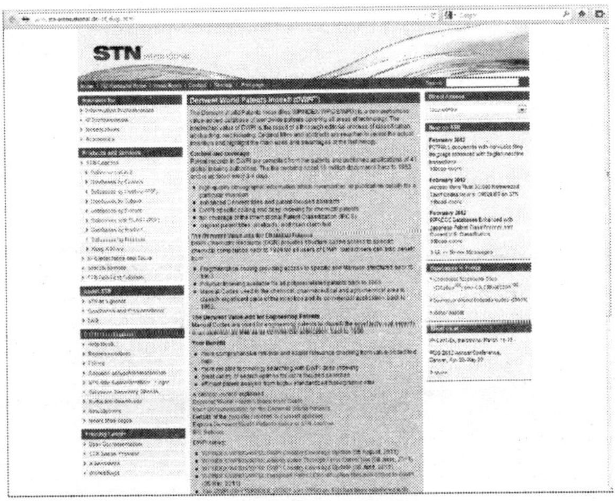

b. Patent and trademarks database of US

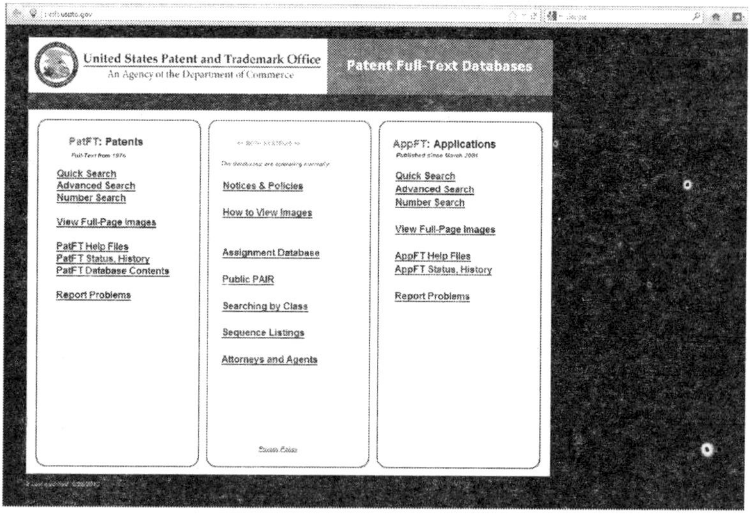

Science news : It is an intellectual activity designed to decipher information about the natural world and to understand the life's mysteries. It is evolving every day. One always wants oneself to be abreast of recent developments which one can get through the online science magazines.

Example :

a. Online Science daily magazine.

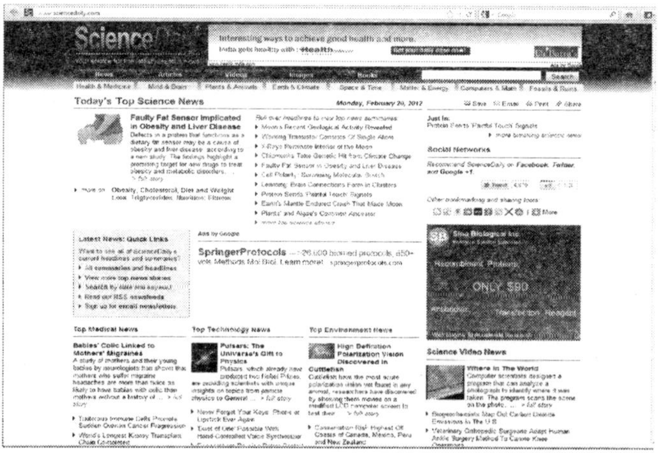

b. Electronic science news

Blogs : It is a personalized electronic journal published on the web comprising of posts displayed in chronologically reverse order. It is the work of a single individual.

Example:

a. Catalogablog discusses about problems as well as perspectives of library catalogues.

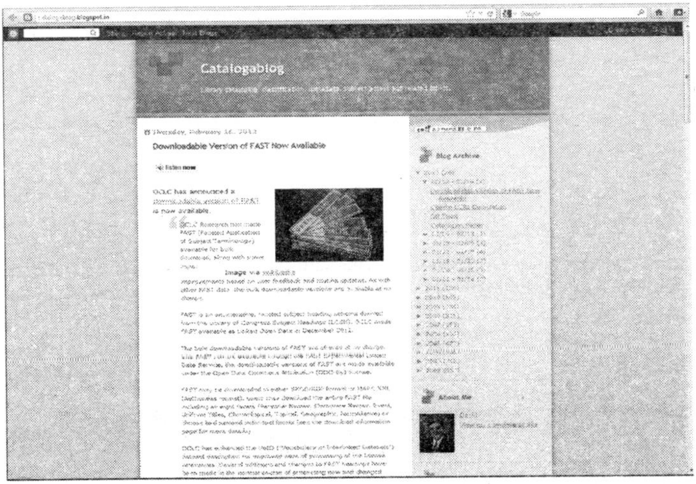

b. The Digital librarian discusses about the emerging trends in digital library

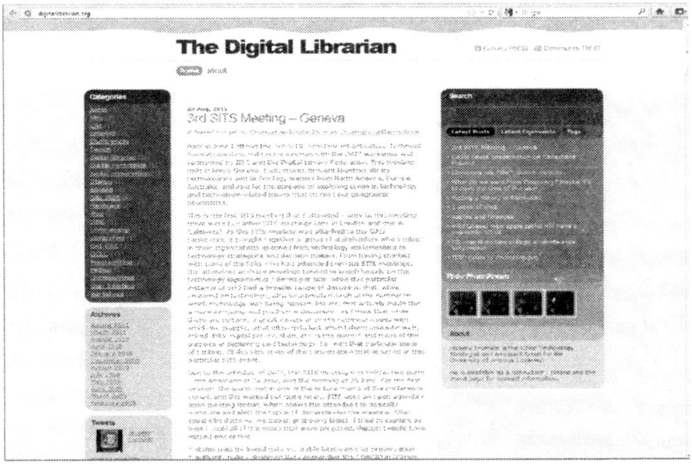

Academic Search engines : It is a search engines tool useful in an academic setting for finding and accessing articles in academic journals, or in repositories, archives, or other collections of scientific and other articles

Example:

a. Bielefeld Academic Search Engine

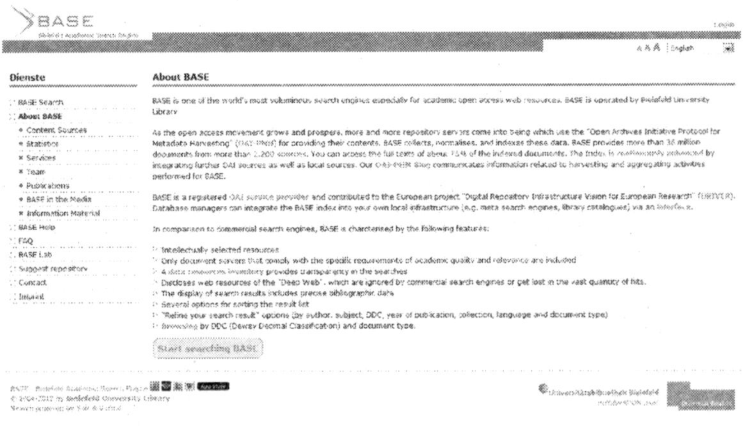

b. Search engine for open full-text arts & humanities journal articles

Software : There are online repositories of software from where desired software can be obtained free of cost.

Example:

1. Online open software repository filehippo

2. Open source software Sourceforge

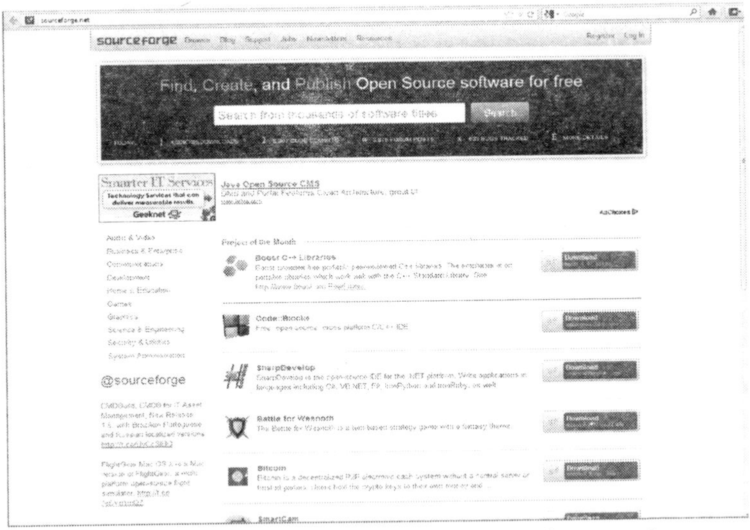

Thesis and dissertations : Thesis or dissertations are the documents submitted for presenting an author's research work and findings. There are online archives of thesis and dissertations hosed by the institutions.

Example:

1. Networked digital library of thesis and dissertations

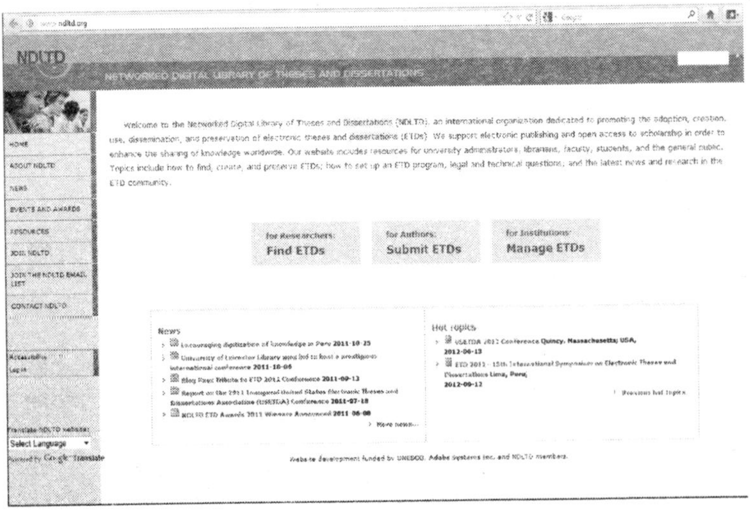

2. Thesis repository of VirginiaTech library

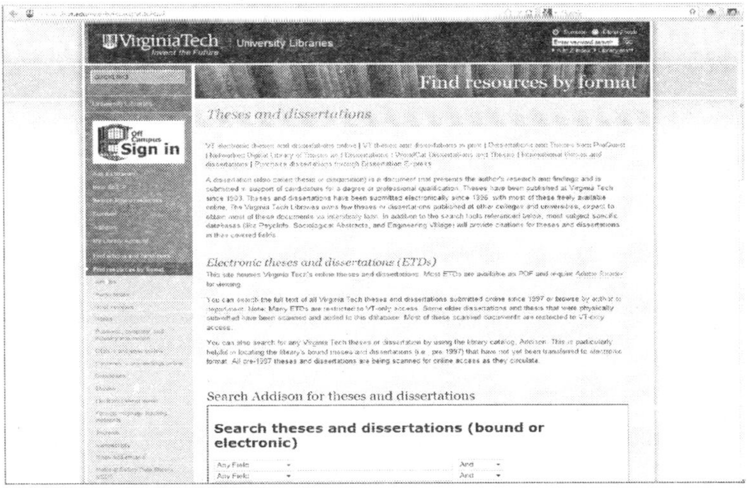

Institutional resources : These are the resources of an organization or institution hosted on the web. In India, all the important institutes have their archives.

Example:

a. NISCAIR online repository

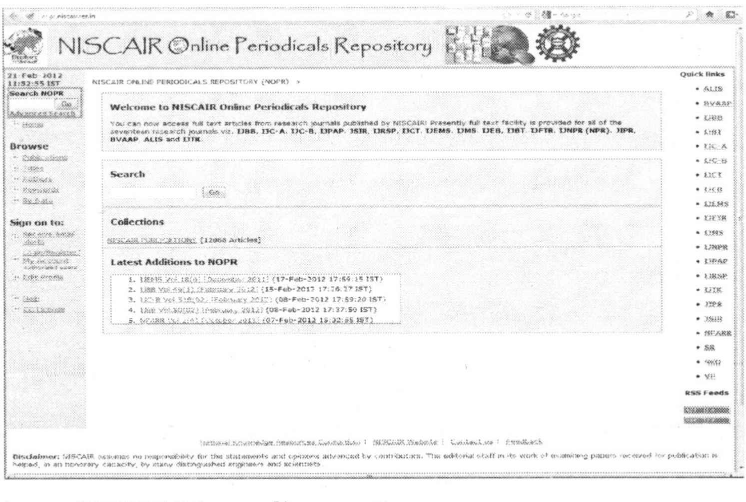

b. DESIDOC journal's repository

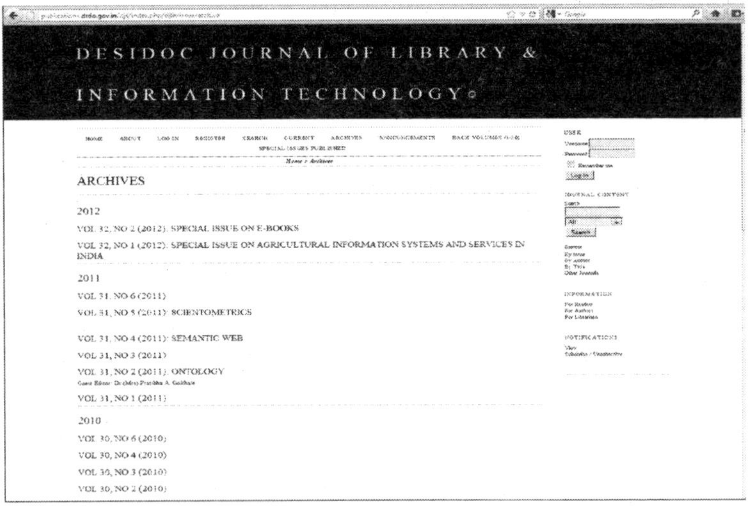

1. Databases, datasets and collections

Abstracting & Indexing databases : They are the collection of records relating to a specific subject domain. Bibliographic databases, abstracts and indexes are now available online.

Example:

1. Scopus abstract and citation database

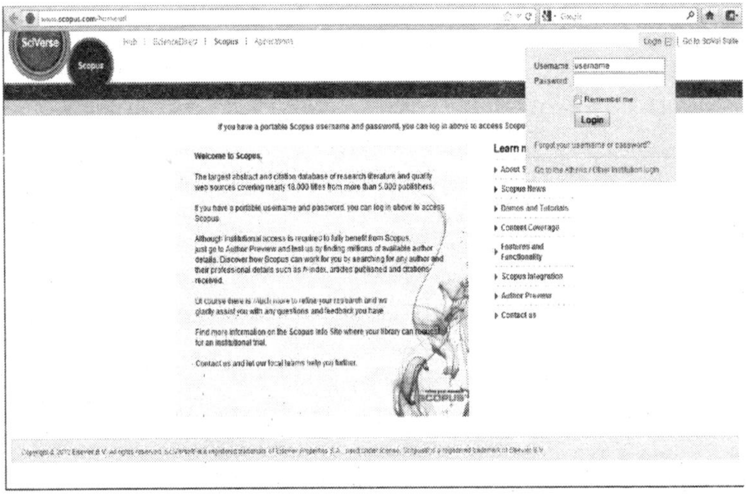

2. Database of medicine

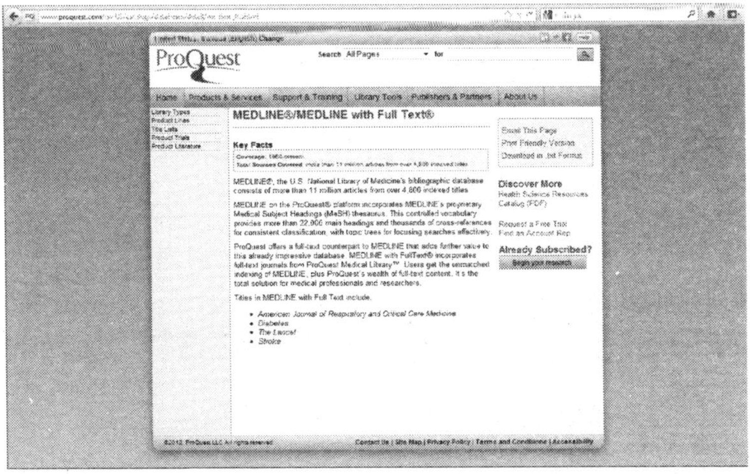

Digital collections : It consists of poly-media websites that contains variants of media viz. Text, graphics and video. The hosted sites consist of ad-ons or plug-inns through which one can use the same. They are mostly software independent offering a visual landscape to web information.

Example :

a. Nine planets multimedia gallery

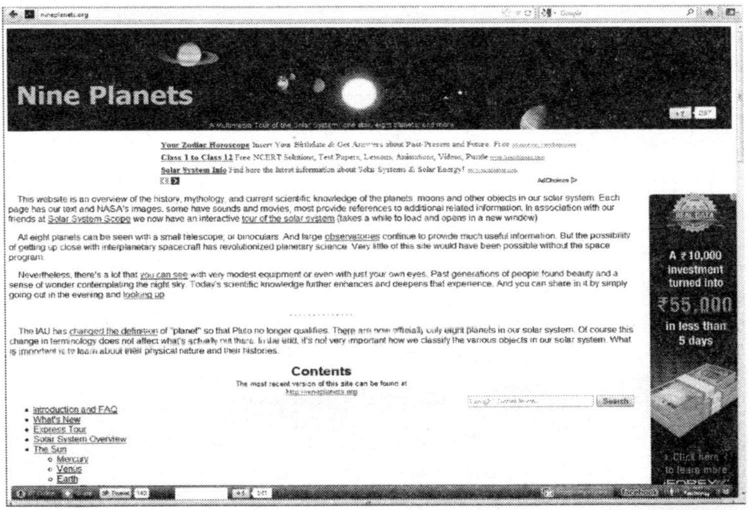

b. NASA Multimedia gallery

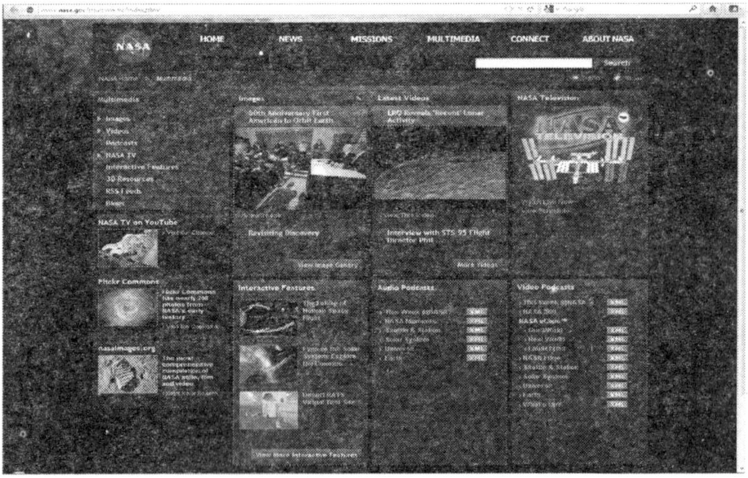

Equipments/ Products : These websites contain product details and specifications. Anyone can look for the desired product, compare with the other products before purchasing and even go for online shoppings.

Example:

a) Online shopping at retails direct

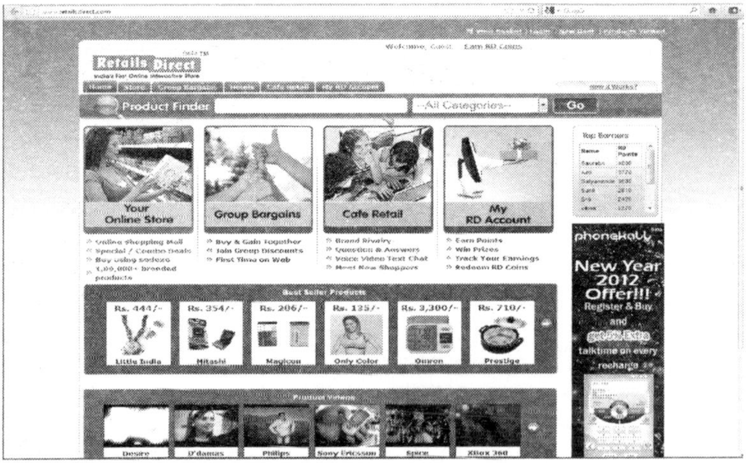

b) Online books and publications of Oxford

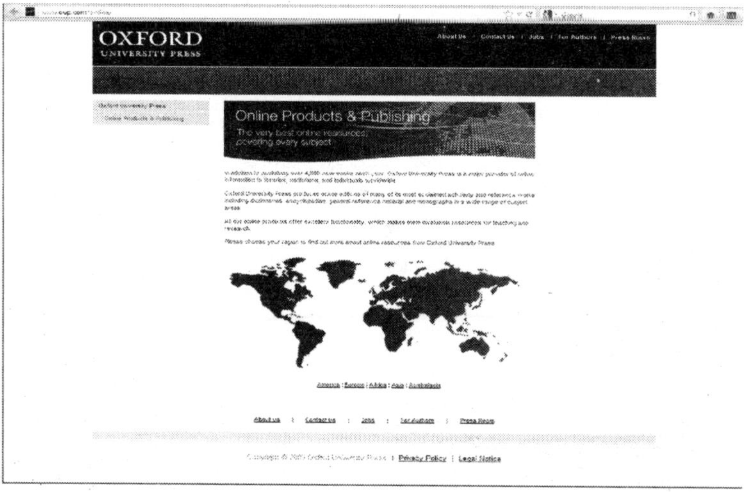

Library catalogues : Catalogue is a tool representing the documents in libraries. These holdings can be searched by author, title, subject or keywords. Online catalogues are an exemplary tool for resource sharing. It can be used to scan through the catalogues of other libraries also.

Example:

a) Library of congress online catalog

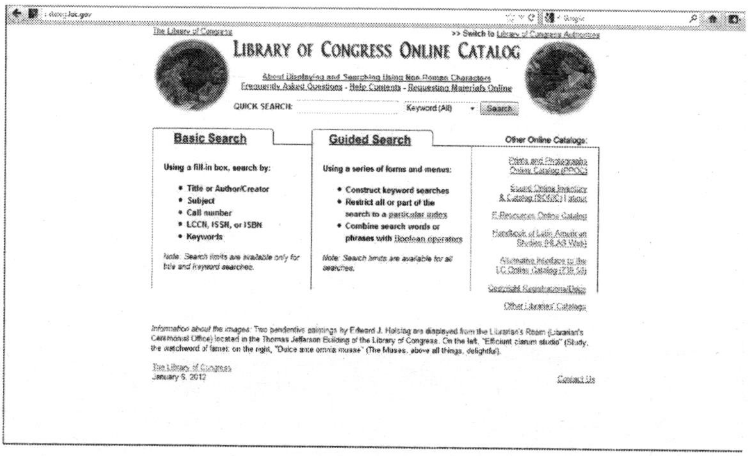

b) Gateway to library catalogues - Libdex

Subject gateways : They are essentially online libraries containing links and pages on a variety of categorized topics. Each subject gateway contains a great deal of information on its given subjects. It may contain a variety of information such as full text documents, resource guides, bibliographies, directories, mailing lists and newspapers, links to other websites, news about new new items or events, and so on.

Example:

a) BUBL link of library science resources

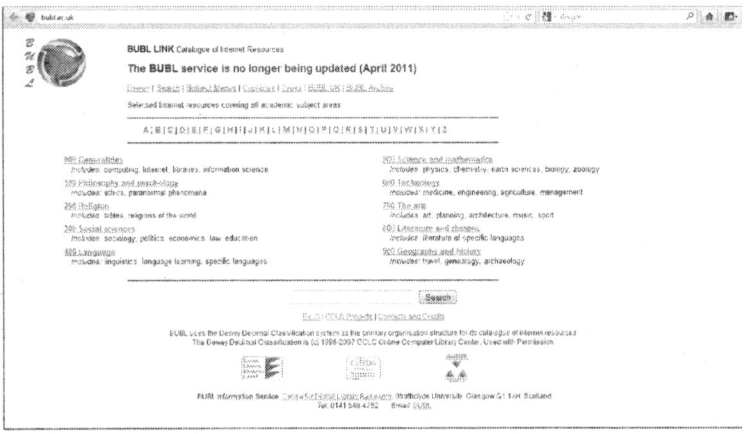

b) Renardus multi-subject gateways

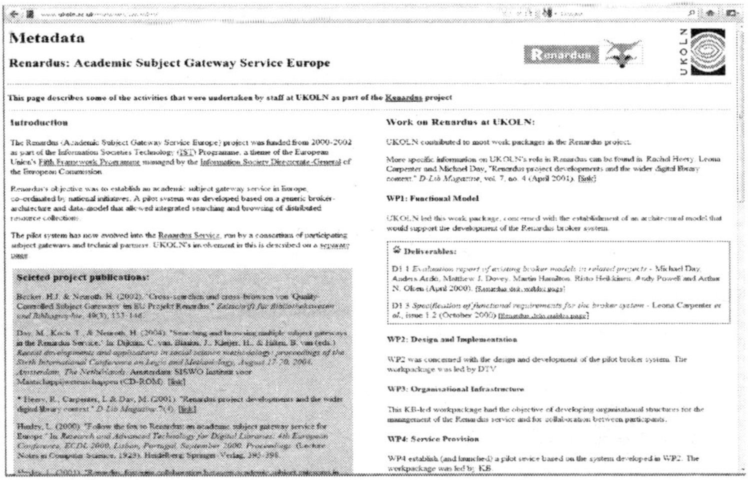

1. Books & reference sources

E-books : An e-book is an electronic representation of a book usually a parallel publication of a print copy, but occasionally "born digital". Also, referred as paperless book, e-book is read on specially-designed devices such as PDA (Personal digital assistant).

a. Sage e-books

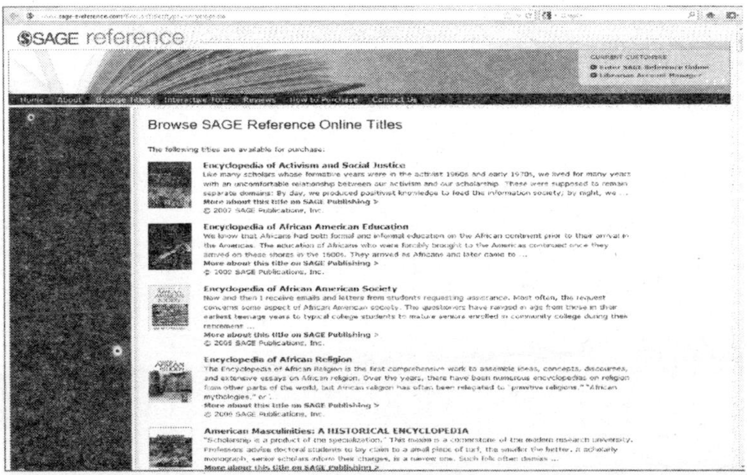

b. Springer e-books

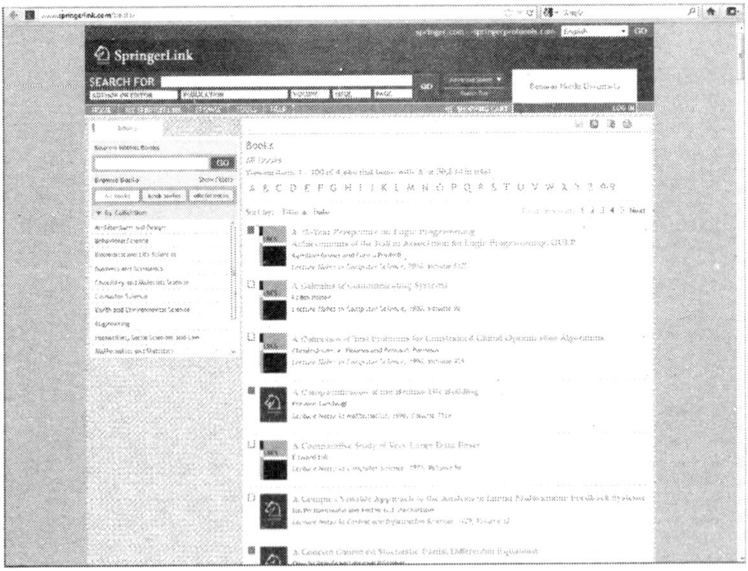

1. Online reference sources

(a) Open access encyclopedia

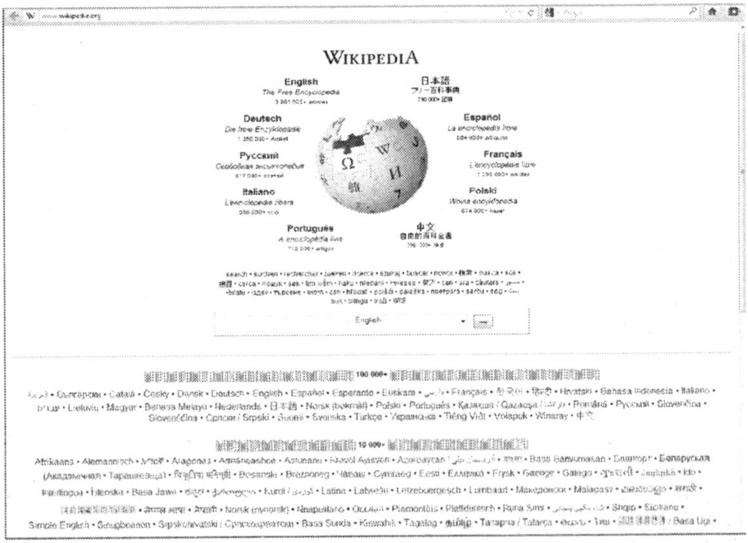

(b) Online dictionary

2. Organization and people sources

Employment and career sources : It is a service designed for both job seekers and recruiters. It is a connecting link between jobs and the companies. It facilitates accepting resume from any part of the world to be posted on the web.

i. Sarkari naukri website, that hosts all the government jobs

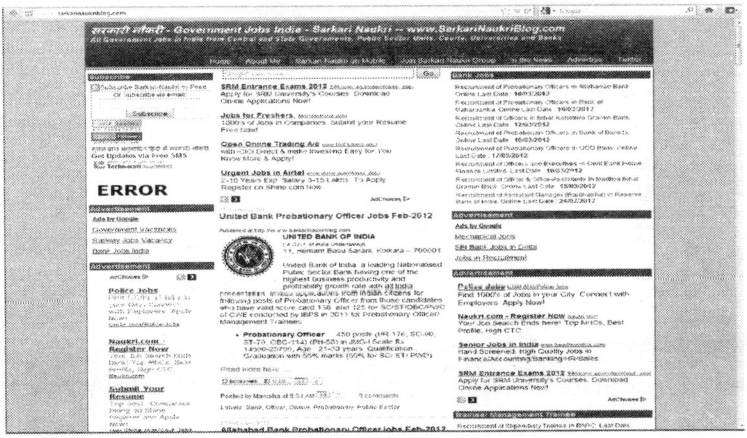

ii. Customized job search engines

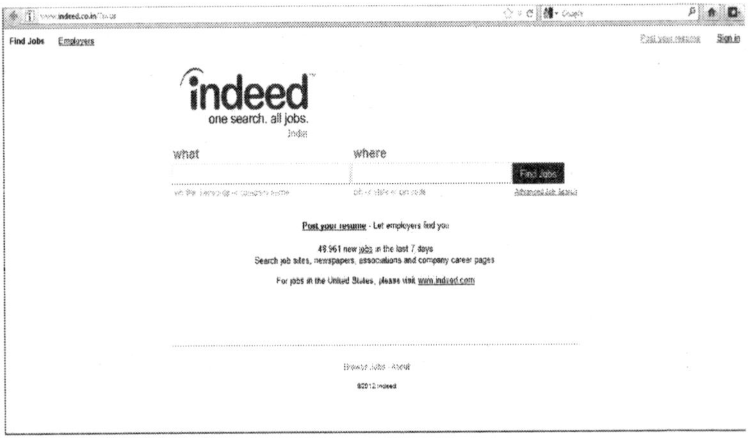

Forums : They are online platform for the professionals who have common objectives and are linked to each other by their practices. It is used for discussing problems and posting ideas on any topic.

Example :

a. Forum for library science professionals - lislinks

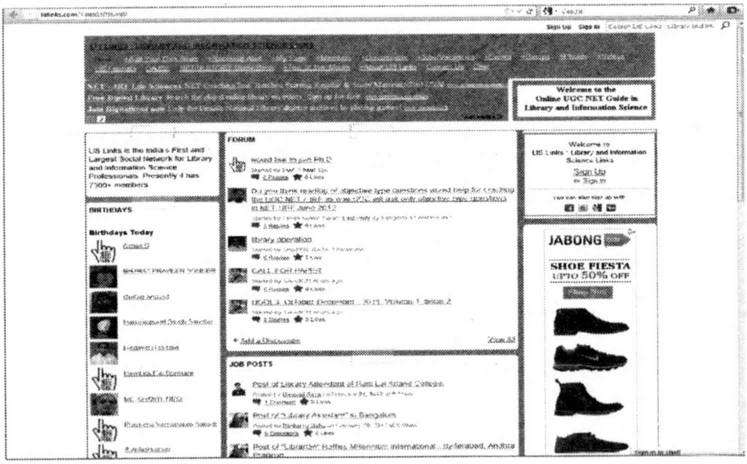

b. Forum for discussing software related issues SQA forum

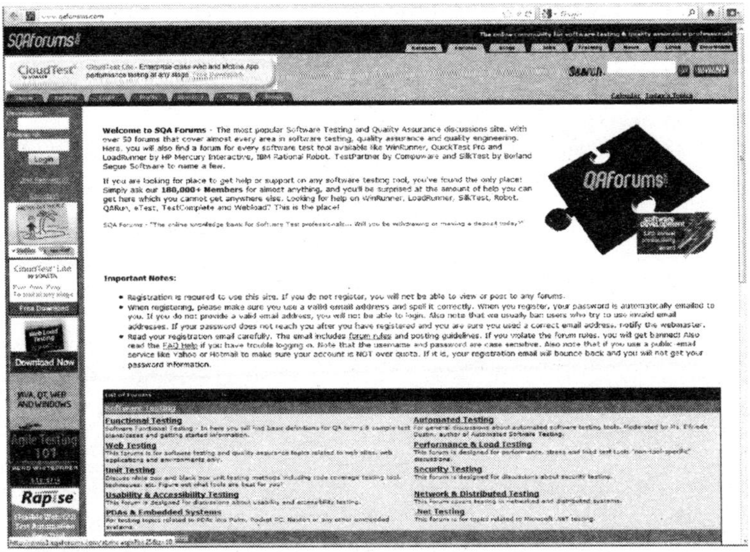

People directories : They are the web based directories of people engaged in various operations across world who can share their feelings on any concerned topics. Some of the online public directories are:

a. Professional networking site- linked in

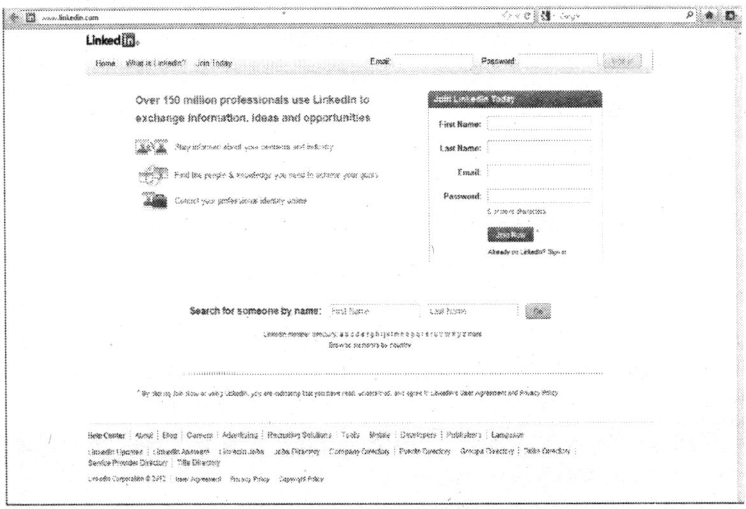

b. Professional networking site- Peer Review

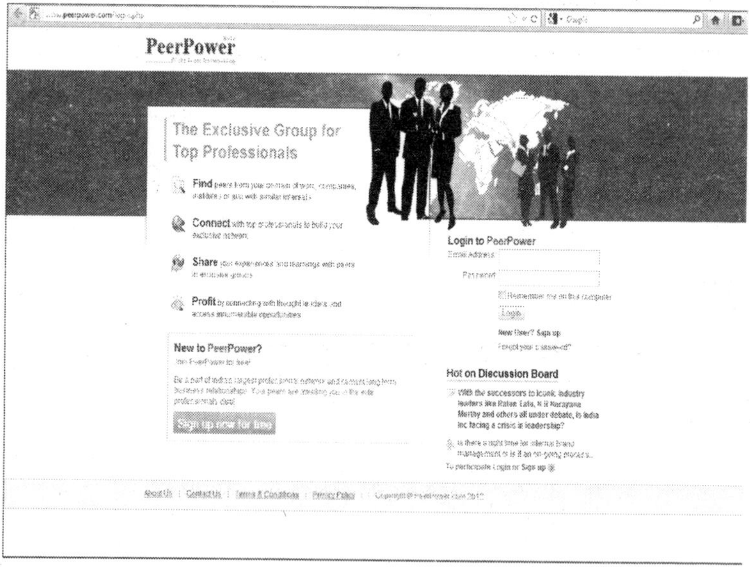

EVALUATION OF WEB-RESOURCES

With an exponential growth in information it has become difficult to find out the requisite information from the information heaps. People are drowning in the information streams with the intervening information channels over the internet. In such a situation there is a need to redesign a system that can monitor the electronic information and the responsibility of the same has been vested in librarians. Long time back with the appearance of electronic resources and internet people had raised questions over the need of librarians when they could get all the information through goggling. However, driven by the needs of information organization, information assessment and to check the validity and viability of the information over internet the role of librarians was felt. In the previous pages we examined all the various Web-resources, now you will find an insight to various tools of evaluation of Web-resources.

Electronic resources

(Singh and Kumar, 2005) has proposed various criteria to evaluate the suitability of electronic resources. It is inevitable to monitor the web based information to ensure reliable and credible flow of information saving resources. The proposed criteria are as under:

Authority

- Firstly, try to find out the knowledge, reliability and truthfulness of the creator of the thought content of the information.
- Then, determine the subject expertise of the author.
- Thirdly, judge the quality and credibility of the available information.
- Then, find out whether the available of information is free from any biasness or not
- Lastly, examine whether the resource belongs to any organization or association. The prestige of the organization and its existing reputation can confirm its authority.

Scope

- Determine the scope of the thought content along with its limitations and omissions.
- Determine whether the extent of subject area is covered adequately or not?
- Determine the retrospective coverage of electronic resources

Accuracy

Objectivity, Correctness, proper referencing and professional sponsorship are mark of information accuracy.

Currency

We need to determine how frequently Web-resources are updated with current information.

Navigation and design

Functionality is of prime importance in a web-resource evaluation. One needs to ask the following questions. One needs to determine that following features are available in a Web-resource.

- Enough internal links
- Updated links and resources
- Logical navigation through the resource
- Relevance of external links to the topic
- Ordered and structured presentation of contents.
- Version of Web content (text based or multimedia)
- User friendly overall design

Audience

Here we need to determine the level of audience or the user group for which the content of web-resources has been written.

Quality of writing

Last but not the least; evaluate the basic spelling and grammatical competence as well as minimal use of jargon. Clarity in discussing complex ideas is desirable.

Electronic databases

(Singh and Kumar, 2005) have proposed various criterias for the evaluation of electronic databases:

Authority

Firstly, one should try to determine the affiliation of the author as well as the popularity of the database producer.

Scope

One should try to find out the statement of the scope of the database as well as the depth of the coverage of the material.

Reliability

One should see whether the database is technically reliable and well compiled with information taken from the valid sources of information.

Accuracy

One should look for the level of quality of writing and editing. Also the presence of bibliographic references to authoritative sources must be verified.

Currency

Currency and timeliness add value to the resources. A user should be cautious about the date of posting, date of revision for getting more current information.

Format

Does the format allow documents to be viewed and downloaded in a variety of formats, such as text or PDF.

Technical Infrastructure

One should try to see whether the product is compatible with existing technical infrastructure of the library or not.

Terms of agreement under the license

One should find out the licensing requirements and the liabilities. Also the restrictions placed on access, copying and distribution and the number of users who can access the product and download the document.

- Cost of the database
- Overlapping

  One should try to find out whether the existing product overlaps with other databases or not.
- Quality of Indexing
- Trials of database

Abstracts

Abstracts are the prelude to the thought content of any article of an electronic journal. It saves quality time ensuring readers that the relevant information is there in the article. Some of the determinant factors for the evaluation of abstracts are:

Readability

- Readability ensures that the abstractor has expressed the content in lucid and concise manner. The sentence length is measured and the number of syllables per word is counted.
- Number of formulae has been put forth to count the number of syllables per word and to measure the length of sentence.

  Flesch Reading Ease Score

  Flesh-Kinacid Grade Level

  Gunning Fog Index

Accuracy

It is used to study the extent to which the information summarized is accurate and truly represents the original document.

Exhaustivity

One should try to find out the extent to which abstract consists of the original piece of information.

Brevity

It can be achieved by reducing the redundancy which is the characteristic of all languages (Borko and Bernier, 1975).

Density

It is the coefficient of the brevity and exhaustivity of the abstract- provided that all relevant information is included. As the length of the abstract lessens, its density grows, provided that the quantity of information remains constant. (Koltay, 2010)

Clarity

It includes the vocabulary and grammatical structure of the abstract (Pinto and Lancaster, 1999)

REFERENCES

1. International Encyclopedia of Information and Library Science. (2003). London: Routledge
2. Encyclopedia of Library and Information Science (2010) New York: CRC Press
3. Choudhary, G.G. (2001) Information sources and searching on the world wide web. London: LA
4. Fecko, M.B. (1997) Electronic resources: acess and issues. London: Bowker-Saur
5. Lesk, M. (1999) Practical digital libraries: books, bytes and bucks. London: Morgan Kaufmann
6. Lankes, D. ...[et al.] (2000) Digital reference service in the new millennium: planning, management and evaluation. London: Neal-Schuman
7. Thulasi, K. NCSI (www.ncsi.iisc.ernet.in/raja/netlis/iirml/kt1.ppt) (Accessed on 8 Feb 2012)
8. Rubin, Richard E. (2004) Foundations of library and information science. New York: Neal-Schuman
9. Singh, S.P. and Kumar, Krishan (2005) Special libraries in the electronic environment. Delhi: BookWell
10. Pinto, M. and Lancaster, F.W. (1999) Abstracts and abstracting in knowledge discovery, Library Trends, 48(1), pp. 234-248.
11. Borko, H. and Bernier, C.L. (1975) Abstracting Concepts and Methods, New York: Academic Press
12. Koltay, Tibor (2010) Abstracts and Abstracting: a genre and set of skills for the twenty-first century.Oxford:Chandos.
13. Web references/ screenshots:
    i. www. Nap.edu/catalog.php?record-id=13333 (Accessed on 21 Feb, 2012)
    ii. thompsonreuters.com/products_services/science/science_products/a-z/index (Accessed on 21 Feb, 2012)

iii. slideshare.net (Accessed on 21 Feb, 2012)
iv. scribd.com (Accessed on 21 Feb, 2012)
v. jstor.org (Accessed on 21 Feb, 2012)
vi. online.sagepub.com (Accessed on 21 Feb, 2012)
vii. stn-international-de/dif_dwpi.html (Accessed on 21 Feb, 2012)
viii. path.upsto.gov (Accessed on 21 Feb, 2012)
ix. sciencedaily.com (Accessed on 21 Feb, 2012)
x. esciencenews.com (Accessed on 21 Feb, 2012)
xi. catalogablog.blogspot.in (Accessed on 21 Feb, 2012)
xii. digitallibrarian.org (Accessed on 21 Feb, 2012)
xiii. filehippo.com (Accessed on 21 Feb, 2012)
xiv. sourceforge.net (Accessed on 21 Feb, 2012)
xv. ndltd.org (Accessed on 21 Feb, 2012)
xvi. lib.vt.edu/find/by/formay/eds.html (Accessed on 21 Feb, 2012)
xvii. nopr.niscair.res.in (Accessed on 21 Feb, 2012)
xviii. publications.drdo-gov.in/ojs/index.php (Accessed on 21 Feb, 2012)
xix. scopus.com/home.url (Accessed on 21 Feb, 2012)
xx. proquest.com (Accessed on 21 Feb, 2012)
xxi. nineplanets.org (Accessed on 21 Feb, 2012)
xxii. nasa.gov (Accessed on 21 Feb, 2012)
xxiii. retailsdirect.com (Accessed on 21 Feb, 2012)
xxiv. oup.com/online (Accessed on 21 Feb, 2012)
xxv. catalog.loc.gov (Accessed on 21 Feb, 2012)
xxvi. libdex.com (Accessed on 21 Feb, 2012)
xxvii. sage-ereference.com (Accessed on 21 Feb, 2012)
xxviii. springerlink.com (Accessed on 21 Feb, 2012)
xxix. Wikipedia.org (Accessed on 21 Feb, 2012)
xxx. Dictionary.com (Accessed on 21 Feb, 2012)
xxxi. Sarkarinaukroblogspot.com (Accessed on 21 Feb, 2012)
xxxii. Indeed.com (Accessed on 21 Feb, 2012)
xxxiii. Lislinks.com (Accessed on 21 Feb, 2012)
xxxiv. Sqaforums.com (Accessed on 21 Feb, 2012)
xxxv. Linkedin.com (Accessed on 21 Feb, 2012)
xxxvi. Peerpower.com (Accessed on 21 Feb, 2012)

9
Information Literacy

"Knowledge is knowing .... or knowing where to find out."

— Alvin Toffler

Information literacy is the competency for diagnosing the information need, to figure out how information is organized, spot the most suitable sources of information for a given need, locate those sources, evaluate them critically and share that information. Information literacy is of prime value because users are surrounded by heaps of information in discrete formats.

In the 21st century the generated information has been flooded with data smog. There is more than simply an information overload. It is not that there is lack of information rather there is too much of data difficult to make out the information clearly from the existing pool of information. Like normal smog the conditions for data smog is intentional. We are not in a position to gaze clearly for the requisite information due to virulent advertisements, ideological pronouncements and infotainment products. We are pounded by data exclusively devoted to dull our senses and distract people from clear and sound thinking on pivotal aspects.

Most of the scholars have used various terms for this stage of information in society like: Infollution and Information pollution. The contamination of supply of information through redundant, unsolicited, irrelevant and low-value information due to useless and undesirable information leads to the state of information pollution. To keep a check on the seepage of information as well as the challenging information pollution there is an urgent need of information literacy. Scholars have given various opinions on the topic depending upon their nature of study and research.

According to ALA, (1998) to be information literate, a person must be able to recognize when information is needed and have the ability to locate, evaluate, and use effectively the needed information. Gilton (1994) opines that compared with library literacy, information literacy is more than searching through an online catalog or other reference materials because information literacy is not a technique, but a goal for learners.

Darch et al. (1997) argues that information literacy requires an awareness of the way in which information systems work, of the dynamic link between a particular information need and the sources and channels required to satisfy that need. National Forum on Information Literacy views information literacy s the ability to know when there is a need for information, and to be able to identify, locate, evaluate, and effectively use that information for the issue or problem at hand.

According to Unesco, information literacy is a basic human right in the digital world as it empowers individuals "in all walks of life to seek, evaluate, use and create information effectively to achieve their personal, social, occupational and educational goals

HISTORY OF INFORMATION LITERACY

The history of information literacy traces its roots to 1950s. The term was first used by Paul Zurkowski in the 70s to fetch people's attention engaged in newly emerging technical environments. Now the concept has been taken as mainstream of concern area by the information specialists and scientists.

The concept has now been made public worldwide with the efforts of the American Library Association and National Forum for Information Literacy. In the 21st century the concept has become the centre of attraction as a true global phenomena drawing interest from all sectors and continents.

Goals of information literacy

- Determination of the breadth and nature of information needed
- Access effectively and efficiently the needed information
- Critical evaluation of information and its sources
- Optimal and effective use of information for accomplishing ones task.
- Realization of economic, legal and social issues encompassing the information use to access and use information ethically and legally.
- To differentiate between various types of available information:
  (a) Scholarly and Popular
  (b) Primary and secondary
- Awareness of fair use and copyright
- Understand the issues of plagiarism and piracy

NEED OF INFORMATION LITERACY

- Judge the credibility of information.
- Acceptance of authoritative texts in the classroom or home library
- Reliability of information available on the World Wide Web.
- Acquisition of competencies of information literacy.
- Increasing role of ICT in libraries and information centers
- Emergence of Internet as an unavoidable need for institution of higher learning and research.

- To make the users competent enough for retrieving precise and relevant information as per their needs.
- Delivery of the right kind of information services to the right users at the right time, demands for well structured Information Literacy and Competency Programs.

COMPONENTS OF INFORMATION LITERACY

i. Tool literacy : It is the ability to understand and use tools based on current information technology relevant to education and professional life.

ii. Resource literacy : It is the ability to know about the form, format, location and access methods of available information resources.

iii. Research Literacy : The ability to understand and use the IT based tools relevant to the work of today's scholars and researchers.

iv. Critical Literacy : The ability to evaluate critically the intellectual, human and social strengths and weaknesses, potentials and limits, benefits and costs of information technologies.

v. Emerging Technology Literacy : The ability to adapt, understand, and evaluate the emerging technologies and make use of the continually emerging innovations in IT.

vi. Basic Literacy : These are the elemental literacy to impart skills of reading, writing, speaking, listening, counting, calculating, perceiving and drawing

vii. Library Literacy : Libraries and information literacy are complementary to each other. Library performs a range of specialized functions for its user which they cannot use it at its level best if they do not possess the necessary skills.

viii. Media Literacy : It includes an understanding of the many different types of media and the purposes for which they can be used

ix. Visual Literacy : It is the link between Media Literacy and Technology Literacy. Media images and sound are end products created using the tools of digital technology. It is the skills and learning needed to view visual and audio/visual materials skeptically, critically, and knowledgeably

x. Technology Literacy : It is the development of opportunities to use technological tools to create their own information artifacts — in print, on the screen, and online.

SPECIFICATIONS OF INFORMATION LITERACY

Specifications are the lucid set of requirements meant to be satisfied during practice to maintain uniformity and an international standard. To control the proceedings of information literacy worldwide ALA has set forth two major guidelines:

Information Literacy Standards

Standards	Indicators
Information literacy standards	
a) The person who is information literate accesses information efficiently and effectively	1) Recognizes the need for information
	2) Recognizes that accurate and comprehensive information is the basis for intelligent decision making
	3) Formulates questions based on information needs
	4) Identifies a variety of potential sources of information
	5) Develops and uses successful strategies for locating information.
b) The person who is information literate evaluates information critically and competently	1) Determines accuracy, relevance, and comprehensiveness
	2) Distinguishes among fact, point of view and opinion

Standard	Indicators
	3) Identifies inaccurate and misleading information.
	4) Selects information appropriate to the problem or question at hand.
c) The person who is information literate uses information accurately and creatively.	1) Organizes information for practical application
	2) Integrates new information into one's own knowledge
	3) Applies information in critical thinking and problem solving
	4) Produces and communicates information and ideas in appropriate formats

Independent learning standards

Standard	Indicators
d) The person who is an independent learner is information literate and pursues information related to personal interests	1) Seeks information related to various dimensions of personal well-being, such as career interests, community involvement, health matters and recreational pursuits
	2) Designs, develops, and evaluates information products and solutions related to personal interests.
e) The person who is an independent learner is information and appreciates literature and other creative expressions of information	1) Is a competent and self-motivated reader.
	2) Derive meaning from information presented creatively in variety of formats.
	3) Develop creative products in a variety of formats.
f) The person who is an independent learner is information literate and strives for excellence in information seeking and knowledge generation	1) Assesses the quality of the process and products of personal information seeking.
	2) Devise strategies for revising, improving, and updating self-generated knowledge.

Social Responsibility Standards

g) The person who contributes positively to the community and to society is information literate and recognizes the importance of information to a democratic society.	1) Seeks information from diverse sources, contexts, disciplines, and cultures. 2) Respects the principle of equitable access to information.
h) The person who contributes positively to the community and to society is information literate and practices ethical behavior in regard to information and information technology.	1) Respects the principles of intellectual freedom. 2) Respects intellectual property rights 3) Uses information responsibly.
i) The person who contributes positively to the community and to society is information literate and participates effectively in groups to pursue and generate information.	1) Shares knowledge and information with others 2) Respects other's ideas and backgrounds and acknowledges their contributions 3) Collaborates with others, both in person and through technologies, to identify information problems and to seek their solutions.

(***Source:***www.ala.org/ala/aasl/aaslproftools/informationpower/InformationLiteracyStandards_final.pdf)

Information Literacy Standards for Higher Education

I. IL person determines the nature and extent of the information needed.	1) IL person defines and articulates the need for information. 2) IL person identifies a variety of types and formats of potential sources of information. 3) IL person considers the cost and benefits of acquiring the needed information. 4) IL person reevaluates the nature and extent of the information need.

II. IL person accesses needed information effectively and efficiently.	1) IL person selects the most appropriate investigative methods of information retrieval systems for accessing the needed information. 2) IL person constructs and implements effectively designed search strategies. 3) IL person retrieves information online or in person using a variety of methods. 4) IL person refines the search strategy if necessary. 5) IL person extracts, records, and manages the information and its sources.
III. IL person evaluates information and its sources critically and incorporates selected information into his or her knowledge base and value system.	1) IL person summarizes the main ideas to be extracted from the information gathered. 2) IL person articulates and applies initial criteria for evaluating both the information and its sources. 3) IL person synthesizes main ideas to construct new concepts. 4) IL person compares new knowledge with prior knowledge to determine the value added contradictions or other unique characteristics of the information. 5) IL person determines whether the knowledge has an impact on the individual's value system and takes steps to reconcile differences. 6) IL person validates understanding and interpretation of the information through discourse with other individuals, subject-

	area experts, and/or practitioners.
	7) IL person determines whether the initial query should be revised.
IV. IL person, individually or as a member of a group, uses information effectively to accomplish a specific purpose.	1) IL person applies new and prior information to the planning and creation of a particular product or performance. 2) IL person revises the development process for the product or performance 3) IL person communicates the product or performance effectively to others.
V. IL person understands many of the economic, legal and social issues surrounding the use of information and accesses and uses information ethically and legally.	1) IL person understands many of the ethical, legal and socio-economic issues surrounding information and information technology. 2) IL person follows laws, regulations, institutional policies, and etiquette related to the access and use of information resources. 3) IL person acknowledges the use of information sources in communicating the product or performance.

(*Source:* www.ala.org/ala/acrl/acrlstandards/standards.pdf)

INFORMATION LITERACY MODEL

Brian Ferguson in Information literacy: a primer for teachers, librarians and other informed people has laid down the information literacy model on the methodologies for the implications of information literacy.

The Model

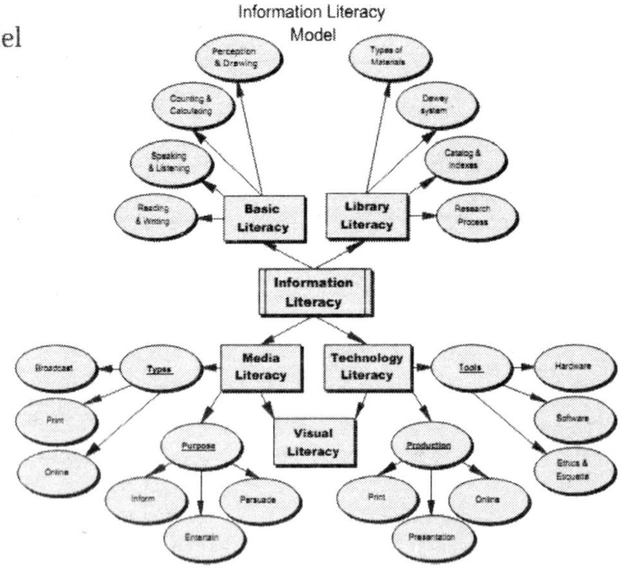

INFORMATION LITERACY METHODS

The different methods of information literacy can be represented as below:

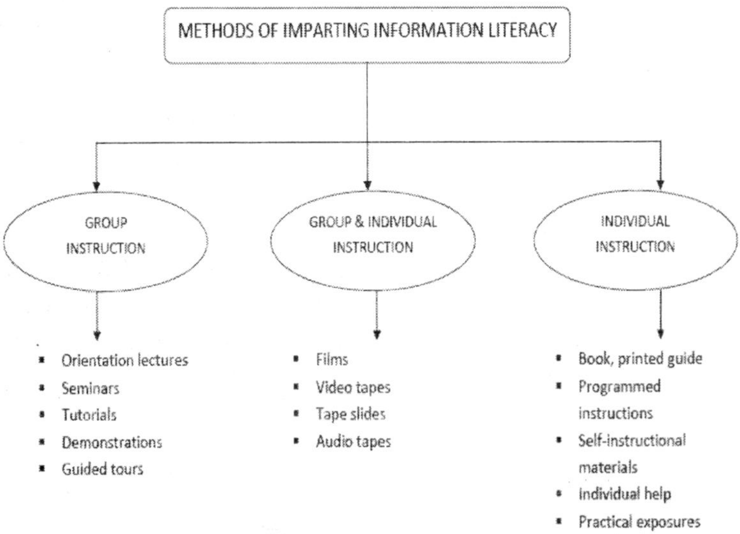

Barriers to information literacy

- Lack of awareness
- Lack of initiatives
- Financial constraints
- Lack of tools and techniques
- Lack of infrastructure
- Lack of co-operation
- Technological constraints

For the information literacy to suffice there is urgency to frame an information policy.

Information policy comprises all the laws, regulations and public policies that encourage discourage or regulate the creation, storage, usage and communication of information. During late 70s or early 80s governments were concerned with the notion of information policy. The genesis of the term traces its root to the activities that began under the name of propaganda in the First World War.

National Information Policies

A national information policy is a set of decision taken by the government, through appropriate laws and regulations to develop infrastructure and plan for information transfer activities in order to satisfy the information needs of the country.

Some of the core issues which need to be addressed through an information policy in India are:

User needs : All activities and programs are to be based on the needs of the users. Different user categories have different needs and in order to fulfill them a careful assessment is necessary.

Resources : Information resources are available in varied range of formats. Indigenously published materials like books, journals, newspapers are deposited in four libraries in India (Delivery of books and newspaper act, 1956). For other materials there is a need of a National information Policy

Information technology : Information technology holds the key to success in modernizing information services. India is perhaps at the first stage of development in the application of information technology. It is only through an enlightened information policy that IT can be enforced.

Institutional resources : Information institutions comprises libraries, documentation and information centres. Also, other type of institutions is likely to come up in future. In such a condition only a national information policy can establish a proper grid of institutions.

Finanacial resources : A national information policy is needed to identify and frame suitable guidelines to allocate finance to this sector

- Marketing of products and services
- Standardisation of library and information science practices and education.

REFERENCES

1. Breivik, P. Student learning in the information age. Oryx press, 1998
2. Bruce, C.S. Seven faces of information literacy. AUSLIB press, 1997
3. Bruce, C.S. and Candy, P. (eds) Information literacy around the world: advances in research and progress, Centre for information studies, Charles Sturt university, 2000
4. Oman, J.N. Information literacy in the workplace, Information Outlook (June): 33-43
5. Debons, A. Foundations of Information Science. In Information: An integrated view. Boston, Mass:G.K. Hall,1980
6. International Encyclopaedia of Information and Library Science. (2003). London: Routledge
7. Encyclopaedia of Library and Information Science (2010) New York: CRC Press
8. Rubin, Richard E. (2004) Foundations of library and information science. New York: Neal-Schuman
9. Gilchrist, Alan (2009) Information Science in transition. London: CILIP.

10. N. Moore (1997) The information policy agenda in East Asia. Journal of Informatio Science 23(2), 139-47
11. Orna, E. (2004) Information Strayegy in practice Gower, Aldershot
12. Eason, K. (1988) Information technology and organizational change London: Taylor and Francis
13. ALA website www.ala.org/ala/acrl/acrlstandards/standards.pdf Accessed on 29 Jan 2012.
14. Marchand, D.A. (2002) Information orientation. Oxford :OUP
15. Saulles, M. de Information (2007) literacy among UK SMEs: an information policy gap, Aslib proceedings 59(1)

10

Knowledge Management

"All knowledge is connected to all other knowledge. The fun is making the connections" — **Arthur Aufderheide**

Knowledge management is a conscious discipline that strives to apply the personal store of knowledge for the accomplishment of organizational goals. It is an eclectic discipline which rests on the centrality of the fact that an organization's cherished resource is the knowledge and skills possessed by its people. Consequently, the amplitude of an organization's performance among other factors rests on how effectively its people are able to create and share new chunk of knowledge around the organization as well as are able to use it to its best effect. It is general misconception among people that knowledge management is all about managing knowledge. However, the endeavour of knowledge management is not to manage all knowledge rather the knowledge inevitable for the organization. In a nutshell, good knowledge management relates to possession of the right knowledge, in the right place at the right time.

ORIGIN OF THE CONCEPT

Knowledge management as a percipient discipline

evolved out of brainwork of Peter Drucker (1970s), Karl-Erik Svieby (1980s) and Nonaka and Tekuchi (1990s). The period witnessed abrupt economic, social and technological changes in the working of companies. New opportunities emerged and competition increased with globalization. Companies started downsizing, merging and reengineering their resources. Most of them started focusing on the usage of network and computer technology. However, it could not yield hardly any fruits of success that led to increasing prices, smaller companies and people no longer knew what they knew. On closer inspection, companies felt that it was their wrong approach to knowledge management i.e. focuses on technology which misled them. In mid90s most of the world's leading companies widely acknowledged that their competitive advantage was due to their knowledge assets like, workers skills, customer relations and innovative measures. Excellence in business provoked other companies to follow the trend and knowledge management emerged as a core business objective.

DEFINING KNOWLEDGE MANAGEMENT

There have been various approaches to define the term. Some of the most prominent are:

- **Abell & Oxbrow, tfpl Ltd, 2001** opines that knowledge management is the creation and subsequent management of an environment, which encourages knowledge to be created, shared, learnt, enhanced, organized and utilized for the benefit of the organization and its customers
- On the other hand, **Peter Drucker** argues that Knowledge is power, which is why people who had it in the past often tried to make a secret of it. In post-capitalism, power comes from transmitting information to make it productive, not from hiding it.
- Similarly, **IBM** thinks that knowledge management is not about data, but about getting the right information to the

right people at the right time for them to impact the bottom line.

- **Nonaka & Takeuchi, 1995** views knowledge management as the capability of an organization to create new knowledge, disseminate it throughout the organization and embody it in products, services and systems.
- **Office of thee-Envoy, 2002** argues that knowledge management is a relatively young corporate discipline and a new approach to the identification, harnessing and exploitation of collective organizational information, talents, expertise and know-how.
- Contrary to the above arguments, **David J Skyrme, 1997** opines that knowledge management is the explicit and systematic management of vital knowledge and its associated processes of creating, gathering, organizing, diffusion, use and exploitation. It requires turning personal knowledge into corporate knowledge that can be widely shared throughout an organization and appropriately applied.
- According to **Encyclopedia of library and information science, 2010** knowledge management is the deliberative and systematic co-ordination of an organization's people, technology, processes and organizational structure in order to add value through reuse and innovation.

PROSPECTS OF KNOWLEDGE MANAGEMENT

The opportunities offered by knowledge management cannot be confined to a singular domain. Some of the prospects are:

- Developing inimitable knowledge
- Safeguarding competitive hold and organization's continuity
- Making the organization independent of its employee

monopoly over his/her inherited knowledge

- Developing a common platform for sharing the skills viable for the common goal o0f practice

KNOWLEDGE MANAGEMENT PROCESS

Knowledge management process broadly involves activities like creating, capturing, refining, storing, managing and disseminating the knowledge.

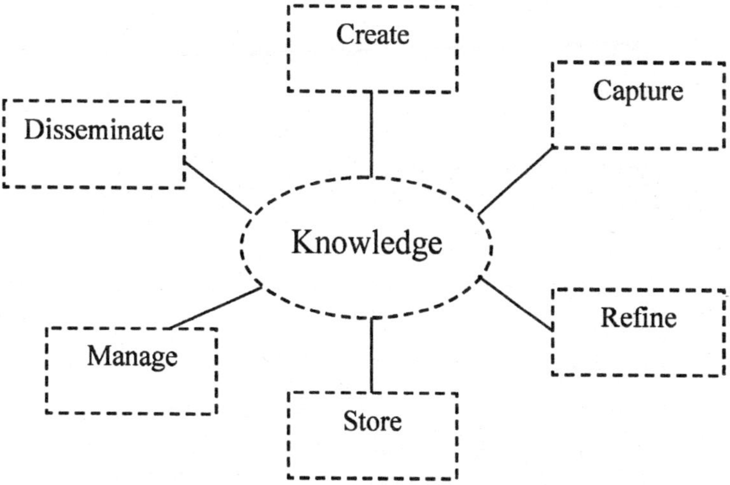

Knowledge Creation

It is a process which involves the conversion of tacit to explicit knowledge. At first Knowledge audit is conducted to identify knowledge needs, knowledge resources and knowledge flows. Further opportunities have to be provided to generate new knowledge.

Knowledge capturing

It is a process where new body of knowledge identified and captured.

Knowledge refining

In this process knowledge is placed in such containers or

into such context which can be easily used.

Knowledge storing

The new chunk of knowledge is stored in repository

Knowledge managing

Here the knowledge is reviewed and evaluated to judge its accuracy and relevance

Knowledge disseminating

Lastly the new body of knowledge is made available at all times to anyone.

Although the knowledge management process seems very simple and easy one yet various policies and processes has to be pre-framed before its implications. Some of the issues are:

1) Knowledge capture: for the identification and capturing knowledge
2) Knowledge transfer: for transferring knowledge among and between various sources and forms
3) Knowledge retention: for retaining organizational knowledge
4) Content management
5) Enabling communities
6) Knowledge culture
7) Knowledge partnerships
8) Knowledge capital
9) Business activities

KM versus traditional IM

It is a general misconception among the savants, who consider KM as just old wine in new bottle. According to them KM was just a new name like information science or documentation for the libraries. In such a situation it is needed to study the phenomenon comparatively with traditional IM.

S.N.	Information Management	Knowledge Management
1.	It deals with explicit knowledge.	It deals with tacit and implicit knowledge
2.	It is concerned with classifying, codifying and transferring knowledge	It relates to identification, creation and distribution of knowledge
3.	It requires tools like schedules, index, databases, computers etc.	It deals with skills or know-how to manage knowledge
4.	It is material-oriented	It is man-oriented
5.	It emphasizes on enquiries to repositories	It emphasizes on collaboration and sharing
6.	It provides good productivity for efficiency	It increases productivity for innovation
7.	It emphasizes on structured or formal information/knowledge.	It emphasizes on unstructured or informal information/ knowledge.
8.	It is concerned with information external to the organization	It is concerned with internal information.

KM TOOLBOX: INVENTORY OF NEW TOOLS

There are various sets of tools and techniques through which ones inherent knowledge can be shared. Knowledge management recognizes that almost all the works presently involves *"knowledge work"* and so all staff are *"knowledge workers"* whose jobs involves major chunk of their knowledge. In every organization creating, sharing and using knowledge at its optimal level are the core activities. It would be a disingenuous labour to put forth various tools as they are in plenitude and various literatures are available. Henceforth it is fair to study the modern tools currently in play.

Knowledge banks (web databases)

They are the secured repositories of stored knowledge held at one central location shared through websites and toolkits. They are built according to the user's requirements and are designed to provide data or advice at any point of time irrespective of location.

Crowd sourcing

It is the act of sourcing tasks to an undefined group of professionals and skilled personnel traditionally performed by specific individuals. It leads to complex problem solving and generation of fresh ideas by anyone around the world.

Knowledge café

It is an informal group of people having an open and creative discussion on issues of mutual interest.

Knowledge marketplace

It is a market space developed for outsourcing ones knowledge on some charges or free of cost. It identifies areas what people know and what they need to know on any subject who keeps them appropriately connected.

Crowd funding

Crowd funding is a branch developed on the lines of crowd sourcing which involves collective cooperation, attention and trust by people for fundraising via internet. It is dedicated for various purposes like charity, disaster reliefs, and political campaigns.

Open innovation

Open innovation is an exemplar issue that assumes that organizations and institutions should employ its internal and external ideas as well as strive to nurture their output with the optimal implication of their intellectual wealth. Corporate bodies should also try to applaud and promote sharing of one's tacit knowledge.

Cloud bookmarking

It is a collaborative tool for social classification of available online sources by identifying broad areas and classifying online resources according to the need and disseminating the same in a form easily assimilated to a larger group at a single platform.

Cloud sharing

They are online tool for sharing ones information in cloud by mounting the information on available repositories. Some of the available repositories are: Storegate, Amazon S3, Flip drive, Google docs, Opendrive, dropbox etc. They act like online storage device. We can secure and customize the features of the same who can browse and edit the same.

Document repositories

Most of the institutions and organizations are now hosting their scholarly as well as scientific works through their hosted repositories. They are providing a platform to submit ones work for wider use independent of any sponsoring body or funding agencies.

Electronic bulletin boards

They are online discussion boards aimed at capturing informal knowledge. They are engaged in generation and transfer of knowledge and emboldening its sharing and collaboration.

Search engines

They are the tools employed by knowledge managers or information professionals to search the information available on the internet. Effective searching is proportional to the search terms or query formulation characterized by a search technique.

RSS

They are the software programs that provide automated access to the nascent information published on the internet. Users have to register for feeds and the new content is automatically received in the feeder.

Instant messaging

They are very handy tool designed to communicate or chat online. It is a platform for informal sharing of ideas and knowledge

Community of practice

It is targeted at networking people who have common interest in a specific area of competence or knowledge, who are eager to work and learn together to develop and share that knowledge.

Collaborative filtering

It is a collaborative process where any document or knowledge is filtered by anyone evaluating its authority and authenticity before adding to the existing pool of knowledge.

Social networking

It is an online service or platform that focuses on creating social relations among people who have a common interest. This service consists of a representation of each user (user's profile), user's social links and a range of additional services. They are mostly web-based and medium to communicate or interact through internet.

Online community

It is a community without walls located virtually in networked environment. Users can be the part of any community of their interest by performing membership ritual. Users can also express and share their knowledge.

Crowd voting

It is a technique where anything can be voted virtually via internet. It is a pivotal tool to collect people's opinion on any problem.

Groupware

They are the programs that help people work together collectively while located remotely from one another.

After Action Reviews

It is a tool explored by US army widely used in organizations and institutions to jot down the lessons learnt during or after an activity or project.

Knowledge harvesting

It is a tool used to capture and document expert knowledge and disseminate it to others.

White pages

It helps people to get knowledge of other people of the organization or institution who have knowledge and expertise for a particular task or event.

Exit interviews

It is a tool used to capture the knowledge and skills of departing employees.

Library tools

Various tools are used in libraries for sharing tacit knowledge like digital libraries, e-documents, library consortia, online catalogues and databases.

Knowledge management in libraries

While the business world is changing in the new knowledge economy and digital age, libraries of all types are undergoing drastic changes also. The new role of libraries in the 21st century needs to be as a learning and knowledge center for their users as well as the intellectual commons for their respective communities where, to borrow the phrase from the Keystone Principles, "people and ideas interact in both the real and virtual environments to expand learning and facilitate the creation of new knowledge." As a learning organization, libraries should provide a strong leadership in knowledge management. Unlike those business organizations whose goal for knowledge management is for competitive advantage, most public, academic, and research libraries, with the exception of company libraries (which may be known or called corporate libraries, special libraries, or knowledge centers), have a different orientation and value. Instead of competition, internal use only, and little sharing of knowledge with others outside, the most important mission of public, academic, and research libraries is to expand the access of knowledge for their users. Charged by this mission, libraries should aim their knowledge management goal high. Below are examples of what libraries can do to improve their knowledge management in all of the key areas of library services:

Knowledge resources management

Because of the exponential growth in human knowledge in a variety of formats, libraries need to develop their resources access and sharing strategies from printed to electronic and digital resources in concert with their mission and charges. Restricted by limited funding, technology, staff, and space, libraries must carefully analyze the needs of their users and seek to develop cooperative acquisition plans to meet these needs. The changing concept from "ownership" to "access" and from "just in case" to "just in time" should be the goal of a sound resources development strategy.

An integrated online public access catalog (OPAC) with both internal and external resources as well as printed and other formats of knowledge should be developed and maintained. Useful websites and knowledge sources should be regularly searched and selected from the Internet and included in OPACs. A system for the reviewing and updating of these resources should be performed. Going beyond explicit knowledge, libraries should also develop means to capture all that tacit knowledge that is of importance to their users, their organizations, and to the internal operation of libraries. The web site of each library should serve as a portal for all sources of selective and relevant knowledge and information whether explicit or tacit, whether on site or remote, and in all formats.

The term "portal" has been defined by Michael Looney and Peter Lyman as "a means of gathering a variety of useful information resources into a single, one-stop Web page, helping the user to avoid being overwhelmed by info glut or feeling lost on the Web." In the current digital and networked knowledge age, the size of information resources on the Web is growing exponentially. No one really knows exactly how many Web pages are on the Internet because new Web pages are added every second.

The latest statistics of Internet hosts numbered close to two billion and is growing fast at the speed of 25% from 1/2001 to 1/2002. Most of the frequently used Internet search engines have also expanded their index sizes by leaps and bounds. For examples, according to the November 11, 2004 report of the Search Engine Watch, Google claimed to have indexed 8.1 billion Web pages; MSN: 5.0 billion Web pages; Yahoo: 4.2 billion Web pages; and Ask Reeves: 2.5 billion Web pages. In a 1999 study by Lawrence and Giles, each search engine may cover only 15% of the Web resources at any given time. Combined coverage of search engines is estimated at 42 percent of the relevant resources. It is also very frustrating that many of the results found—in the tens of thousands of hits—are irrelevant. One has to comb the large number of findings in order to find the few relevant pieces of information. Still, information on the Web can be very useful if only we can employ advanced artificial intelligent tools to surf the Internet and to select, find, arrange, classify, and automatically deliver the needed information to each user based on his/her special interests and needs. Many such new knowledge management systems are under development and testing and hold promise for greatly enriched knowledge resources, improved user services, and the more efficient use of knowledge for creation and decision-making.

Universities and research organizations are themselves knowledge reservoirs. These highly valued intellectual assets, regardless of whether they are explicit or tacit, should be inventoried, archived, indexed, frequently updated, and made accessible in digital form. In addition, the traditional, time-honored methods of cataloging and classification are barely adequate to handle the finite number of books, journals, and documents, but are inadequate to deal with the almost infinite amount of digital information in large electronic databases and on the Internet. Using the Dublin Core metadata and the Cooperative Online Resources Catalog (CORC) has been a new approach to capture Web information by cooperative efforts. Other new methods such as data mining, text mining, content management, search engines, spidering programs, natural language searching, linguistic analysis, semantic networks, knowledge extraction, concept yellow pages, and such techniques in information visualization as two-dimensional or three-dimensional knowledge mapping, etc. have been a part of recent developments in knowledge management systems.

Resources sharing and networking

Libraries have a long tradition of resources sharing and networking. These have been greatly expanded by the rapid development of computer, telecommunication, networking, and digital technologies since the 1960s. In the U.S. it is very common for libraries to be a member of several consortia at the same time for various types of cooperative work and resources sharing. The best examples of these are the OCLC Online Computer Library Center and OhioLINK (Ohio Library and Information Network). The CORC project of OCLC should be especially useful for libraries to cooperatively capture digital resources of all types, describe them in a standard format, and make them easily searchable by users.

The successes of most of these examples in resources sharing and networking are largely the result of the full cooperation and participation of all member libraries without selfishness. Large and major libraries must take the lead in such an endeavor. Supports in policies and funding from the government or parent organizations are also critically important. Experiences indicate that all libraries, regardless of size and specialties, have been benefited by library cooperation and resources sharing.

Information technology development

To facilitate the implementation of knowledge management, a well-designed and operational knowledge management system should be in place. Latest information technology should be used as an enabler. In this regard, the library director should consider him/her self as the chief knowledge officer of the entire organization and should work together with the CIO, heads of the planning department, the computer and information technology center, the human resources management department, the finance department, etc. to design and develop such a system. Such a knowledge management system should be built on existing computer and information technology infrastructures, including upgraded intranet, extranet, and Internet, and available software programs to facilitate the capture, analysis, organization, storage, and sharing of internal and external information resources for effective knowledge exchange among users, resource persons (faculty, researchers, and subjects specialists, etc.), publishers, government agencies, businesses and industries, and other organizations via multiple channels and layers. In recent years, many of the newly developed information technologies for database and information/document management can be utilized in knowledge management; such as, data warehousing, data mining, text mining, content management, knowledge extraction, knowledge mapping, groupware, and information visualization, etc. It was observed by Hsinchun Chen that "since the mid 1990s, the popularity of search engines and advances in web spidering, indexing, and link analysis have 12Knowledge transformed IR systems into newer and more powerful search tools for content on the Internet."

User services

The utmost goal of knowledge management is to provide users with a variety of quality services in order to improve the communication, use and creation of knowledge. As much as possible these services should be tailored to the interest and needs of each user. Information about each user can be obtained by analyzing the records of user registration, surveys, circulation and interlibrary loans, frequently asked reference questions, and the use of e-journal and digital resources, etc. User satisfaction and needs should be collected through periodic users' surveys. The findings should be used for the planning and redesign of library services. It is very important, however, that user's privacy should always be protected. Some of the manual services such as "new publication alert" and "selective dissemination of information," which libraries have been providing, can now be done automatically by employing the "push technology" with great efficiency and convenience. Each library user can also set up his/her virtual "My Library" enabled by library systems and networks for collecting and organizing resources for personal use and to stay informed of new resources provided by the library. The Library and Information Technology Association (LITA) has defined MyLibrary-like services as the number one trend "worth keeping an eye on." It further stated that "Library users who are Web users, a growing group, expect customization, interactivity, and customer support. Approaches that are library-focused instead of user-focused will be increasingly irrelevant."

Human resources management

A great amount of expert knowledge is possessed by library staff and users, both in and outside the libraries. In university and research communities such expertise is abundant and should be inventoried, indexed, and updated regularly and be made searchable and accessible through electronic databases created and maintained by libraries. The knowledge and accumulated experiences of library staff members form the intellectual assets of any library and should be valued and shared. An organizational culture for sharing of knowledge and expertise should be established with appropriate rewards and incentives. Those staff members who share their tacit knowledge and experiences through writing, publishing, lecturing, tutoring, or mentoring should be appropriately recognized and rewarded. An organizational culture which emphasizes cooperation, sharing, and innovation can only be established by strong leadership and commitment from the library director and a shared vision by the library staff. As a learning organization, libraries should allocate annual funding to provide continuing education and staff training to all staff members. Knowledge must be renewed and expanded to prevent it from becoming stagnant.

In the business world, knowledge management has been regarded as strategically important for organizations to gain a competitive advantage over their competitors, to add value to their products, and to win greater satisfaction from their customers. In the library world, there is a lesson to be learned from the business world. Knowledge management is as important for libraries as for the businesses minus the competitive, proprietary, and moneymaking concerns. In fact, libraries have had a long and rich experience in the management of information. Many of such knowledge and skills of librarianship can be applied to knowledge management. For any library to succeed in implementing knowledge management will require a strong leadership and vision from the top administration, which can influence the organization's knowledge sharing efforts in a positive way. As libraries enter the knowledge age of the 21st century, we should not take a back seat in the development of knowledge management. Instead, armed with our professional knowledge and experiences, we should be in the driver's seat. Information technology and systems can provide effective support in implementing knowledge management. Librarians should work together with IT professionals and others to develop the appropriate knowledge management systems. Furthermore, knowledge management should never be viewed as a way to control the process of knowledge creation. In his book, Enabling Knowledge Creation, Georg Von Krogh et al made a strong argument for supporting knowledge creation rather than controlling it. In the process of knowledge creation, every library should strive to be an enabler and facilitator by mobilizing all its efforts and resources. The best knowledge creators are academics. Knowledge creation is best performed by universities. As a learning and knowledge organization, universities should empower their libraries to develop campus-wide knowledge management systems. It is now time for libraries to reposition themselves in the central stage of and as a leading player in knowledge management.

Impediments for KM implementation

Most of the organizations and institutions of 19th century responded to knowledge management solutions focusing entirely on knowledge management technologies. But due to unsatisfactory results, people began to raise questions on the very foundation of knowledge management which they found fanciful that looked great on paper, but in reality did not deliver. Various reasons can be ascribed for poor knowledge management:

- Inapposite use of MIS and IT
- Lack of initiatives of the government

- Unwillingness to knowledge creation and sharing
- Lack of expertise
- Lack of awareness among people
- Lack of policies and practices
- Lack of any National body to control the activities
- Lack of finance

Fahey and Prusak enlist the eleven sins of knowledge management:

- Lack of any working definition of knowledge
- Emphasizing knowledge stock to the determinant of knowledge flow
- Viewing knowledge as existing outside the heads of the individuals
- Not understanding that a fundamental intermediate purpose of knowledge management is to create shared context.
- Paying little heed to the role and importance of tacit knowledge
- Disentangling knowledge for its users
- Downplaying thinking and reasoning
- Focusing on the past and present not on the future
- Failure to recognize the importance of tacit knowledge
- Substituting technological contact for human interface
- Seeking to develop direct measures of knowledge

Role of Librarians in KM Environment

- To know about man, material and money.
- To know about potential sources and its best utilization
- To know about records management, indexing method, databases and thesaurus construction
- To know about competencies, loopholes and prospective

- Literacy extension.
- Efficient and effective time management to utilize time and energy for acquiring knowledge
- Use of different learning methods to absorb key knowledge and learning instantaneously
- Informal networking skills to connect with other resource persons and to understand user needs
- Use of resource investigation skills to decipher knowledge
- Use of IT skills for information recording and dissemination
- Co-operative problem solving
- Flexibility and willingness to try new things and take educated risks

Responsibilities of Librarians in KM Environment

- Providing extensive and highly diverse global organization development support to strategic business unit;
- Spearheading strategic change methodologies to drive systematic improvement and results;
- Developing employee engagement and involvement strategies;
- Diagnosing organizational development issue;
- Leading the development and execution of an organizational learning process and curriculum;
- Leading the external staffing strategy;
- Managing the internal talent review processes; and
- Driving employee satisfaction survey process.

Functions of librarians in KM environment

- Finding, mapping, filtering, packaging and disseminating knowledge;

- Converting tacit knowledge into shared resources;
- Conducting analyses that identify needs, specify resources and anticipate barriers to participation and performance;
- Facilitating the transfer of knowledge to on the job activities;
- Managing organizational change including creating cultures and developing policies;
- Organizing information to have resonance for people at work;
- Developing self-directed learning; and
- Designing and developing systems that transfer ideas to actions at work.

Some of the areas where the role of librarians is inevitable in KM landscape are(Encyclopaedia of Library & Information Science, 2010):

Knowledge officer : They ensure that KM goals are in line with organizational goals and strategies.

Learning officer : They ensure that the organizations acts like a learning organization, improving overtime with the help of accumulated best practices and lessons learned

Knowledge managers : They are responsible for acquisition and management of internal and external knowledge.

Knowledge navigators : They are responsible for knowing where knowledge can be located. They are also referred as knowledge brokers.

Knowledge synthesizers : They are responsible for facilitating the recording of significant knowledge to organizational memory, also called knowledge stewards

Content editors : They are responsible for codifying and structuring content, also called content managers; roles involving capturing and documenting knowledge

- Web-developers
- Electronic publishers
- Intranet managers
- Content managers

Learning-oriented roles : such as trainers, facilitators, mentors and coaches

Human resources roles : developing programs and processes that encourages knowledge oriented culture and behaviours

Help desk activities : It involves delivery of KM and information related to training, also called knowledge support office.

New age competencies for information professionals in KM environment

Library and information profession has undergone drastic changes with times. The influx of IT, ICT technologies as well as seepage of information science has ripened its scope and possibilities. To adept oneself to these changes one has to keep pace with the changes otherwise it will derail us. The winds of change brought by KM environment can be faced by following desirable competencies:

SERVICEABLE COMPETENCIES

a) Breadth and depth of corporate mindset and experience

b) Ability to deal with the vendors

c) Ability to employ ones knowledge and skills in outsourcing services

d) Ability to contribute to competitive intelligence of the parent organization and institution.

e) Ability to manage the content and ensure optimal user satisfaction and usage of services.

OPERATIVE COMPETENCIES

a) Strategic planning

b) Decision making

c) Sound marketing and good public relations

SERVICE ENRICHMENT COMPETENCIES

a) Focus on user needs and expectations

b) User education

c) Information literacy

d) Aptitude for information handling

INEVITABLE SKILLS

a) Effective handling of technologies like A.I. , Experts System Extranet, Intranet, GroupWare, Decision support, Document Management System, Data warehousing/ Mining, Internet, etc;

b) knowledge of organizational development concepts;

c) Expertise in leadership development including succession planning, executive coaching and design of workshops/ interventions;

d) Outstanding oral and written communication skills including presentation, planning and delivery skills;

e) Process consultation and facilitation skills (Accelerated learning and reading, Information filtering and critical thinking skills , brainstorming and creative problem solving).

Challenges for information professionals

- Difficulty in capturing and managing tacit knowledge
- Hesitation in knowledge sharing
- Obsolescence of information
- Rapid change in information technologies
- Financial constraints

- Difficult in identification of KM needs

To sum up, it can be said that we live in a changing world that constantly throws up new challenges. The clever thing to do is to convert these into opportunities. There is no wisdom in being blindly obstructionist or rapaciously greedy. Coming up with creative solutions is what we need most. We shouldn't be diffident about extracting maximum mileage out of our inherent strength so that more LIS professionals can benefit, and that the nation as a whole develops in a more even-handed manner than the current lopsided growth. A creative proactive human approach could simultaneously cure many maladies. If there are common threads running through the talents of all these leaders, they are ones of vision, leadership, advocacy and an evangelical belief in KM as the key to competitive advantage in the knowledge age."

REFERENCES

1. Barclay, R. and Murray P. What is a knowledge management? Knowledge Praxis. http://www.Mediaccess.com/whatishtml,1997 (accessed Dec, 15, 2011)
2. Tang Shannong. Knowledge management in libraries in the 21st century. (Accessed on 15-01-2012) http://www.ifla.org/iv/ifla66/papers/057-110e.htm
3. Thomas H Davenport. The future of Knowledge Management. (Accessed on 18-01-2012) http://www.cio.com/archive/010096-dovenpor-content.html
4. Marriane Broadbent. The phenomenon of knowledge management: what does it mean to the information profession? (Accessed on 20-01-2012) http://www.sla.org/pubs/serial/io/1998/may98/broadben.html
5. Rowley, Jennifer. Knowledge management in the new librarianship: From custodians of history to the gatekeepers to the future. Library Management, 2003, 24(8/9), 433-40
6. Ho, Diem , "Research, Innovation and Knowledge Management", (Accessed on 13-01-2012) http://portal.unesco.org/education/en/files/55811/12015104365Ho_final_versionEN.pdf/Ho_final+versionEN.pdf

7. Abell, Angela & Oxbro, Nigel. Competing with knowledge: the information professionals in the knowledge management age. Library Association Publishing, London 2001

8. Elearn. Knowledge management: Information and knowledge management revised edition Pergamon:Oxford 2009, 76-95

9. Stankosky, Michael Creating the discipline of knowledge management the latest in university research. Butterworth-Hienemann 2005

10. Peraz, E. A successful shot: knowledge management challenge. Online, 26(6) 25-29, 2002

11. Dalkir, K. (2005) Knowledge management theory and practice. Butterworth-Hiensman:Boston , MA

12. Broadbent, M. (1998) The phenomenon of library management: What does it mean to the library profession? Information outlook 2(5): 23-36

13. Hibbard, J. (1997) Knowing what we know. Information week (October): 46-64

14. International Encyclopaedia of Information and Library Science. (2003). London: Routledge

15. Encyclopaedia of Library and Information Science (2010) New York: CRC Press

16. Chaudhary N.B., Acharya P. (2003) Knowledge management: paper presented at the MANLIBNET 5th Annual Convention. March 6-8, 2003, XLRI Jamshedpur.

Index